MERCEDES-BENZ
110 YEARS OF EXCELLENCE

Written and Photographed by Dennis Adler

MBI Publishing Company

First published in 1995 by MBI Publishing Company, PO Box 1, 729 Prospect Avenue, Osceola, WI 54020-0001 USA

© Dennis Adler, 1995

The information in this book is true and complete to the best of our knowledge. All recommendations are made without any guarantee on the part of the author or Publisher, who also disclaim any liability incurred in connection with the use of this data or specific details.

We recognize that some words, model names, and designations, for example, mentioned herein are the property of the trademark holder. We use them for identification purposes only. This is not an official publication.

MBI Publishing Company books are also available at discounts in bulk quantity for industrial or sales-promotional use. For details write to Special Sales Manager at Motorbooks International Wholesalers & Distributors, 729 Prospect Avenue, PO Box 1, Osceola, WI 54020-0001 USA.

Library of Congress Cataloging-in-Publication Data
Adler, Dennis
    Mercedes-Benz color history / Dennis Adler.
      p. cm. -- (MBI Publishing Company enthusiast color series)
    Includes index.
    ISBN 0-7603-0046-1 (pbk.)
    1. Mercedes automobile--History. 2. Mercedes automobile--Pictorial works. I. Title II. Series: Enthusiast color series.
TL215.M4A332   1995
629.222'2—dc20   95-14006

On the front cover: A century plus of progress. At center is the Benz Patent-Motorwagen of 1886, at left is a 1937 540K, and at right is a 1994 600SL.

On the frontispiece: The grille, as much as any other detail, identified the SSK as a Mercedes-Benz.

On the title page: The stunning 540K Special Roadster defined 1930s-era elegance.

On the back cover: Handsome and a strong performer as well, the 300SE Coupe was powered by a 3.0-liter inline six, similar in layout to that used in the 300SL sports cars.

Printed in China

Contents

FOR JEANNE, MY CONSTANT INSPIRATION

Acknowledgments

As the world's first and arguably greatest automaker, Daimler-Benz encompasses so many years, models, and technological achievements that it would require volumes to cover its entire history. In *Mercedes-Benz: 110 Years of Excellence* I have attempted to select the most significant examples from each decade in Benz, Mercedes, and Daimler-Benz history and put them in chronological order, detailing their developmental history, technical achievements, and styling. If we have somehow overlooked one of your favorite models, it was by no means a slight. Every Mercedes-Benz model built is worthy of mention.

As with any historical undertaking, one must follow the lead of those who have preceded us down the path. Mercedes-Benz history has been well documented, and I acknowledge the works of many authors and historians who have published books and articles on this subject: *Mercedes-Benz, the Supercharged 8-Cylinder Cars of the 1930s, Vol. 1*, by Jan Melin; *Mercedes-Benz, the First Hundred Years*, by Richard M. Langworth; *The Star and the Laurel*, by Beverly Rae Kimes; *Mercedes-Benz, a Century of Invention and Innovation*, Lowell C. Paddock, Senior Editor; *The Star,*

May/June 1985, "Past Perfect," by Dennis Adler; *Car Collector & Car Classics*, October 1985, "The Invisible Collector Car," by James A. Harper; *The Star,* November/December 1988, "230SL," by Dennis Adler; *Mercedes-Benz Personenwagen 1886-1984*, by Werner Oswald; *Mercedes-Benz 300SL Art & Color Edition*, by Jürgen Lewandowski; *Mercedes-Benz 300SL*, by Dennis Adler.

The creation of any marque history involves the efforts of many people in addition to the author. The editorial content of this book would not have been possible without the cooperation of my friend, and fellow Mercedes-Benz historian, Frank Barrett, editor of *The Star*, the official publication of the Mercedes-Benz Club of America.

Others who have contributed to the works which make up the content of this book include authors T. C. Browne and the late Dean Batchelor, and from Mercedes-Benz North America, Fred Heiler and archivist Lois Anderson.

My thanks to one and all for taking part.
Dennis A. Adler
Pennsylvania
January 1995

Introduction

Mr. Benz & Mr. Daimler

In the late 1880s, Carl Benz put together the works of some creative engine designers, himself included, bicycle mechanics, and drivetrain innovators; elements, that when properly combined, would change the course of history.

The horseless carriage was a dream that had existed throughout the ages, as far back as Leonardo da Vinci, in his *Codice Atlantico*. The closest thing to a surrey that could actually move under its own power dates back to 1769 and the Cugnot Carriage, a massive three-wheeled wagon powered by a steam engine. A train for two.

As a viable concept, the development of the automobile as a means of personal transportation can be traced to 1885 when Carl Benz opened the doors of his Mannheim workshop and rode around the yard in a three-wheeled carriage powered by a single-cylinder internal-combustion engine.

On January 29, 1886, Benz was granted German patent number 37435 for his invention—the Patent-Motorwagen—recognized today as the first automobile. Had he waited just a little longer, Benz would have had to share that distinction with Gottlieb Daimler.

In the town of Cannstatt, Daimler had received a patent for an internal-combustion engine and, with his protégé Wilhelm Maybach, began construction on a four-wheeled horseless carriage. The Daimler Motorenwagen was introduced at virtually the same time as the Benz three-wheeler. The two most famous men in automotive history had set about a mutual course that would ultimately lead to the merger of their respective companies in the late 1920s. Ironically, at the time, neither Benz nor Daimler knew anything of the other's work, and they lived less than 60mi apart.

Daimler was not as interested in producing horseless carriages as he was in manufacturing the internal-combustion engine in all its permutations, on land, on the sea, and in the air—origin of the now famous "three-pointed star." By the time Daimler Motoren Gessellschaft was formed in November 1890, Daimler and Maybach had developed a public street car, a taxi line, the first motor driven fire engines, power boats, and the first lighter-than-air craft, the dirigible. Here, Daimler (holding pocket watch) is pictured with one of his commercial trucks, circa 1900. *Photo courtesy Mercedes-Benz North America*

By the early 1890s, both Benz and Daimler had moved from experimentation into the production of motorized vehicles. The public, however, didn't exactly beat a path to their doors. We may as well face it: The automobile was an orphan of the Industrial Revolution. Unlike many inventions of the 19th and

20th centuries, there was no accumulated demand for the automobile, at least not for one that was slower than a bicycle, far less reliable than a horse, and for which it was necessary to purchase an explosive liquid called *Benzin* from the local apothecary. Benz nevertheless persevered. By 1900 his Motorwagen had been joined by the Viktoria, Velo, and Ideal models, the world's first production automobiles.

Daimler was not as interested in producing horseless carriages as he was in manufacturing the internal-combustion engine in all its permutations, on land, on the sea, and in the air—origin of the now famous "three-pointed star." By the time *Daimler Motoren Gessellschaft* was formed in November 1890, Daimler and Maybach had developed a public street car, a taxi line, the first motor-driven fire engines, power boats, and a dirigible.

Daimler and Maybach had also developed and patented the first vee-twin engine, a 4-speed gearbox with gated linkage, a jet-type carburetor (still the basis for modern carburetors), and the first motorcar with a front-mounted engine—a significant step beyond the limited styling of the "horseless carriage." That concept was Gottlieb Daimler's legacy. He died in March 1900 at the age of sixty-six, the course of his automotive company steered anew by Emil Jellinek, the Daimler distributor for Austria-Hungary, France, and Belgium.

Jellinek was a visionary who saw the need for faster, more stylish cars. Both Maybach and Daimler's son Paul shared these beliefs and had in fact been working on such a design. But these were conservative times, and the Daimler board of directors had reservations. To persuade them, Jellinek agreed to purchase the first thirty-six cars, with one stipulation, that they be named after his twelve-year old daughter, Mercedes. Improbable as it all sounds, the board agreed to this arrangement. The 1901 models were equipped with a more powerful engine, lower chassis design, stylish, if not trend-setting coachwork, and were named Mercedes. It became the first "modern" motorcar, a pattern that has prevailed, virtually unchanged, almost to this moment—four road wheels, steel chassis, honeycomb radiator in front of the engine, gated gear-change lever, driven rear wheels. Unless something quite drastic changes the way in which we design and power automobiles, this simple formula created almost 100 years ago will still be the basis for the *modern* motorcar well into the next century.

The Benz Patent-Motorwagen is recognized as the world's first automobile. As a viable concept, the development of the automobile as a means of personal transportation can be traced back to 1885 when Carl Benz opened the doors of his Mannheim workshop (recreated in the photograph) and rode around his yard in a three-wheeled carriage powered by a single-cylinder, internal-combustion engine.

CHAPTER ONE

Before the Turn of theCentury:

The 1886 Patent-Motorwagen
and
1898 Benz Ideal

C arl Benz grew up in an era when few ordinary people ventured far from their hometown. Mass transport, when it finally came to be, was the steam locomotive. Personal transportation was powered by hay, and luxury meant a coach-built carriage. To the average person, the concept of driving, let alone owning a car, must have seemed as unlikely in the 1880s as it is to us that someday we might pilot cars that fly above city streets.

Though we celebrate the introduction of the motorcar in 1886 as a turning point in modern civilization, the automobile was not simply and suddenly invented. Although Benz started it all, he did not single-handedly put the world on wheels. More importantly, the Patent-Motorwagen showed what was possible.

Why did Benz choose three wheels instead of four as Daimler used for his Motorwagen? The answer is that Benz did not use the horse-drawn carriage as a basis for his car. Instead, he departed far from it. His tricycle configuration appeared more logical, less complicated, lighter, and easier to steer. This theory reigned until Benz designed the four-wheeled Viktoria, which appeared in 1892.

The Benz Ideal was introduced in 1898 and remained in production until 1902. The four-wheeled model was a traditional Benz *vis-a-vis* (face-to-face) design with seating for four—driver and one passenger in the rear seat, and two passengers in the smaller front seat facing the driver. An arrangement that no doubt made conversation much easier, but driving from the rear seat was more of a challenge.

The Patent-Motorwagen pictured is one of eleven such replicas built by Daimler-Benz AG apprentices for the centenary of the automobile in 1986. It is identical in every detail to the original three-wheeler for which Benz received his January 29, 1886, patent and was built using the same kind of tools and crafts. The Patent-Motorwagen used a simple tubular frame with full-elliptic leaf-spring suspension supporting the rear axle. As the lateral pivot point of a three-wheel design, the front wheel turned on a solidly-mounted axle without springing. The driver steered by turning a hand lever atop the steering column. At the bottom of the column, a gear rack transferred motion via a long rod to a bellcrank at the front-wheel fork. This tiller-type steering was used in one form or another by most 1890s automakers. Benz finally designed an improved steering mechanism, which he patented in 1893 and introduced on the Viktoria.

The Patent-Motorwagen was powered by a water-cooled, single-cylinder, horizontal engine. The piston and cylinder were oriented fore and aft, and displacement was 954cc (58ci). Output was about 0.75hp at 400rpm, sufficient to propel the three-wheeler at speeds up to 10mph. The exposed connecting rod and crankshaft drove an attractively sculpted flywheel beneath the engine and a simple transmission above.

From here power went via belt to a rudimentary differential, thence to both wheels by chain.

The driver started the engine by spinning the flywheel by hand. Ignition was by coil and battery, and Benz had to invent his own spark plug. Fuel flow was adjusted by a knurled handle beneath the driver's seat, while brakes were controlled by a large lever to the driver's left. Benz made several design improvements before putting the three-wheeler into production in 1888, but the basic layout prevailed during its four years of manufacture. It is estimated that about twenty-five were made.

Throughout the 1890s Benz und Cie. produced a variety of four-wheeled models. The very first four-wheeler, the Viktoria, resembled Daimler's first models. In 1893, Benz added the Velo, which was somewhat smaller and less powerful, what history might consider the world's first compact car. In 1898, Benz added the Ideal.

One interesting point about motoring in this era was the cost of an automobile. The Viktoria, for example, sold for $4,500 in the mid-1890s! In 1895, the company produced and sold 134 automobiles, but Benz was falling behind the competition. By 1901, Daimler's new Mercedes models were establishing design and performance marks that Carl Benz refused to even acknowledge. A renaissance at Benz und Cie. in the early 1900s at last brought these two great companies into direct competition, helping to define the emerging automotive market of the twentieth century.

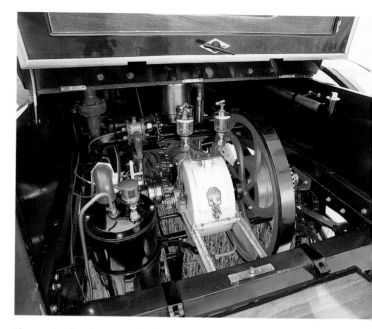

The engine for the Benz Ideal displaced 1,045cc and developed 3hp at 700rpm. By 1902, the engine had been improved to 2,090cc with an output of 8hp at 1000rpm. Although a very stylish form of voiture, by 1902 the Ideal was completely outclassed by the new Mercedes model which would establish the basic parameters for automobile design used to this day.

CHAPTER TWO

Benz & Daimler:

The 1900s and Early 1920s

Gottlieb Daimler succumbed to a worsening heart condition in March 1900, leaving the company to the DMG Board of Directors, his son Paul, Daimler's long time friend and chief engineer, Wilhelm Maybach, and the firm's single largest benefactor, Emil Jellinek.

With the success of the new 1901 Mercedes, production demands began to outstrip the capabilities of Daimler's Cannstatt headquarters. Around 1904, DMG moved to a larger facility in the Untertürkheim district of Stuttgart. Production at the old Cannstatt Werk continued until the building was razed by fire June 10, 1903. Everything including all of the serial numbers and factory records from 1901 was lost.

Although Daimler only produced 35 cars in 1902, the '01 and '02 models introduced many innovations, including the honeycomb radiator, 4-speed transmission, water-cooled rear brakes, and for the time, one of the most powerful engines in the world.

The 1900s marked the beginning of an era when enterprise and progress in the development of personal transportation literally advanced by leaps and bounds, from mere single-cylinder motor-driven carriages to automobiles capable of carrying passengers at 60mph, a speed once thought to be beyond human endurance.

Custom coachwork endowed otherwise conservative Benz models with exceptional styling. One such example was a 1911 90hp chassis fitted with a wooden Skiff body designed by French coachbuilder Henri Labourdette, who pioneered the design and would influence Skiff and boattail coachwork for better than a quarter century. *B. Scott Isquick collection.*

LEFT: This 1902 Mercedes 40hp is arguably the oldest existing Mercedes motorcar in the world, one of only 35 built by Daimler Motoren Gesellschaft at the original Cannstatt factory in 1902. Daimler only produced thirty-five cars in 1902. The '01 and '02 models introduced many innovations, including the honeycomb radiator, 4-speed transmission, water-cooled rear brakes, and for the era, the 40hp motor was one of the most powerful in the world.

The Victoria Touring body, designed by A. T. Demarest & Co. of New York City featured a large rear tonneau with folding top and a removable canvas hood over the driver's compartment. The car had neither windows nor side curtains, consigning it strictly to fair weather driving.

The car pictured, a 1911 Benz Victoria from the Don Ricardo collection, was a special model, with a modified 50hp engine and a full custom body built by A. T. Demarest & Co. of New York City at a cost of nearly $10,000 in 1911. This is the only known example of the 50hp Benz chassis. The 1911 model rode on 920x120mm (36.8x4.8in) front tires and 935x135mm (37.4x5.4in) rear tires, mounted on wooden artillery wheels. The frames were of pressed-steel construction, made of Krupp nickel steel, in-swept in front to ensure a short turning radius.

While Ransom Olds and Henry Ford developed cheap, mass-produced cars between 1900 and 1914—cars which were to drive the price of most automobiles

below $1000—the affluent were privy to such costly *voitures* as the American Underslung (upward of $4,000), the British-built Rolls-Royce Ghosts (with an equally astounding tab), and from Germany, via the Benz Auto Import Co. of America in New York City, the entire Benz line, a selection of four Mannheim-built chassis and sixteen coach-built bodies—perhaps the best motorcars of the era, from either side of the Atlantic.

Benz and Rolls-Royce were the best known imports in America throughout the early 1900s. Benz established American distributorships in New York City, on Broadway between 48th and 49th Streets; in Philadelphia, at Bergdoll-Hall Motor Car Co.; in Atlanta, at the Georgia Motor Car Co.; and in Chicago at Benz Motor Co. on Michigan Avenue.

For 1911, Benz chassis prices ranged from $3,250 for the 18hp model up to $8,500 for the sporty 60hp versions. Mind you, a new Model T Ford sold for only $900 in 1911, and that was a complete car, not a bare chassis! Except for the 60hp models, bodied mainly as sport runabouts, the 45hp Benz was the top

ABOVE: Competition models such as this 1922 Mercedes Targa Florio were among the most impressive motorcars of their time. Named after the race in which the model was entered in 1922, the Targa Florio was built on a massive channel-section steel frame with semi-elliptic springs all around. The 6-cylinder engine drove through a double leather cone clutch and a 4-speed transmission.

LEFT: An example of typical coachwork used in the early 1900s, this 1910 model was bodied as a two-place raceabout. Top speed for this car was around 45mph.

of the line, offering the greatest variety of custom and standard coachwork, with normal body prices from $1,000 to $2,250.

Benz models produced throughout the 1900s grew progressively more modern in appearance, though still more conservative than Mercedes of the same period. Custom coachwork did, however, endow certain

Mercedes models became so popular in America that from 1905 to 1907 they were built in the United States by the Daimler Manufacturing Co. of Long Island City, New York. These cars were known as American Mercedes. The American manufacturing operations were owned by William Steinway, better known for manufacturing pianos. *Photo courtesy Mercedes-Benz North America*

models with exceptional styling. One such example was a 1911 90hp chassis fitted with a wooden Skiff body designed by French coachbuilder Henri Labourdette. Built for American Henry Stetson, this was the most exciting non-racing Mercedes ever produced.

Benz took a commanding lead in motor racing beginning in the early 1900s with such unparalleled models as the 1909-10 Blitzen Benz and later with competition cars like the 1922 Targa Florio. Throughout the period leading up to and after WW I, both Benz and Mercedes models grew in popularity with literally hundreds of different designs between them. By the end of the 1920s, however, these two great independent automakers would be drawn into an alliance that would make them the largest and most important automotive manufacturing company in Europe. Carl Benz would live to see this happen. The inventor of the first patented automobile died in 1929, at the age of eighty-five, three years after the merger of Daimler and Benz.

The new 1901 Daimler models were equipped with a more powerful engine, lower chassis design, stylish, if not trend-setting coachwork and were named Mercedes. It became the first "modern" motorcar, the foundation upon which almost every automobile since the turn of the century has been based; a pattern which has prevailed, virtually unchanged, to this moment—four road wheels, steel (instead of wood) chassis, honeycomb radiator in front of the engine, gate-change gear lever, driven rear wheels, a front seat for driver and passenger, and rear seat for passengers. *Photo courtesy Mercedes-Benz North America*

CHAPTER THREE

The Great Merger of 1926:

The Early Cars of Daimler-Benz and Ferdinand Porsche

Much is to be said for those things that have survived the test of time. Be it a political ideology or an automobile company, to any or to all, time is indifferent. Tastes change, as do political and economic climates. Throughout more than a century, Mercedes-Benz has endured these changes, while many others have not.

"The war to end all wars" left Germany's economy on perilous ground after the 1918 Armistice, and by the early 1920s there were precious few buyers for new and expensive cars. In addition to Benz and Daimler, there was Horch, Opel, Auto Union, Wanderer, and Adler, to name a few. In all, eighty-six German companies were building 144 different models—yet only one German in 280 owned an automobile!

By 1924 Benz and Daimler found themselves forced closer and closer together. In May of that year, the two firms entered into an agreement of mutual interest, a non-competitive and cooperative arrangement that served as a prelude to their merger in June 1926. This marriage of necessity consolidated their engineering and production capabilities into the largest automobile manufacturing company in Germany.

This Mercedes Boattail Speedster was commissioned in 1928 by Howard Isham of Santa Barbara, California, with the coachwork designed and built by the Walter M. Murphy Co. in Pasadena. As far as can be determined, only one Boattail Speedster was ever built on an SSK chassis, and of the entire SSK production, roughly thirty-one cars, only two were bodied outside of Europe and Great Britain; the second, also by Murphy, was a cabriolet built for Zeppo Marx.

A German classic, bodied in France by two Americans, this 1927 Model K is an international model. Thomas Hibbard and Howard "Dutch" Darrin, together as Hibbard & Darrin of Paris, designed and built the body for the striking blue cabriolet pictured. They were also responsible for some of the finest coachwork of the 1920s and early 1930s. Much of Hibbard & Darrin's work for Mercedes took place after the merger of Daimler and Benz. Designing coachwork for the Model K chassis, the talented team created a number of body designs, including a four-door cabriolet, imperial limousine and several two-passenger cabriolet styles.

Though each was successful individually, when Benz und Cie. and Daimler Motoren Gesellschaft became Daimler-Benz AG, they were inspired. The first product of their combined effort, aside from the little-changed, traditional, lower-priced Mannheim and Stuttgart models, was the Model K, introduced in 1926.

Model K

The Model K was more an evolutionary design than a completely new luxury automobile. Based upon the Type 630 Mercedes 24/100/140 PS introduced in 1924, it was principally the work of chief engineer Dr. Ferdinand Porsche and his predecessor, Paul Daimler. Porsche improved upon Daimler's pioneer overhead-camshaft (ohc) 6-cylinder engine design and Roots-type supercharger, giving the massive K models unparalleled straight-line performance. Specified by Daimler-Benz to attain 90mph, it was the fastest standard model of its type in the world.

As to the K's road manners, any change over the 630, however small, would have to be considered an improvement. The 630's stiff underpinnings—semi-elliptic leaf springs at all four corners and cumbersome channel-section chassis—imparted all the character of a truck. The K introduced an improved suspension design on a shorter wheelbase, 134in versus the 630's 147.5in.

With less overall weight on a more responsive suspension, Dr. Porsche was able also to increase the output of Daimler's supercharged six, which had previously made 100hp, unblown, and 140hp with the supercharger engaged. The improved engine made 110hp standard and 160hp blown. The new power came from a higher compression ratio (5.0:1, up from 4.7:1) and better ignition through Porsche's use of two spark plugs per cylinder. With a bore and stroke

of 94x150mm, the K's engine displaced 6.24ltr (381ci). The 630's 4-speed gearbox, with straight-cut gears and a 1:1 ratio in top, was retained.

As a transitional model during the Mercedes and Benz consolidation, the Model K proved to be an excellent luxury alternative to the sporting S, SS, SSK, and SSKL models that followed.

Models S, SS, SSK, and SSKL

The Model S and later SS and SSK models were built on a new drop-center frame with a 133in standard wheelbase. To improve the handling over the Model K, the new design moved the radiator and engine about a foot rearward on the chassis, resulting in better front–rear weight distribution and a lower center of gravity. This lower chassis also encouraged more rakish, open coachwork.

With chassis improvements came more power, 120hp under normal aspiration, 180 with supercharger. The updated engine in the Model S, the single strongest tie to Daimler, had its bore increased from 94 to 98mm. With a 150mm stroke, this brought displacement up to 6,789cc, about 414ci. The SSK—powered by a 170/225hp (increased to 180/250hp in 1929), Roots supercharged inline six—was capable of reaching the magic century mark, a speed that, for the time, every builder of luxury cars claimed to achieve; Mercedes did. Racing versions with higher-compression engines running on Elcosine—an alcohol/fuel mixture used for competition—reached speeds well in excess of 100mph.

Off the track, nearly all Model S body styles were open touring designs but very traditional, severe, and upright in appearance. Besides those from its own factory at Sindelfingen, bodies for Daimler-Benz were built by coachbuilders Erdmann & Rossi, Papler, and Zeitz in Geneva, Switzerland.

RIGHT: The 1927 Model K with restored interior still shows the exquisite upholstery work done in Italy by Castagna, but has been toned down some from the original design. Driver's compartment for the chauffeur is also finely detailed.

Apart from the normal touring bodies were several sport-touring types with cut-down doors and more rakish lines. The best styling on the Model S, however, came from outside Germany. Exotic coachwork from France's Saoutchik included a splendid convertible coupe; Van Den Plas of Brussels built a cabriolet; and an even more stylish cabriolet came from D'Ieteren in Belgium. British imports were mainly bodied by Freestone & Webb in traditional saloon styling, and

Another version of the 1927 Model K is this town car bodied in Italy by Carrozzeria Castagna. This is one of only two examples of the 630K to have been coach-built by the Italian firm. The body styling is typical of Castagna and closely resembles their designs for Isotta Fraschini chassis. The Mercedes-Benz grille is the only identifying characteristic.

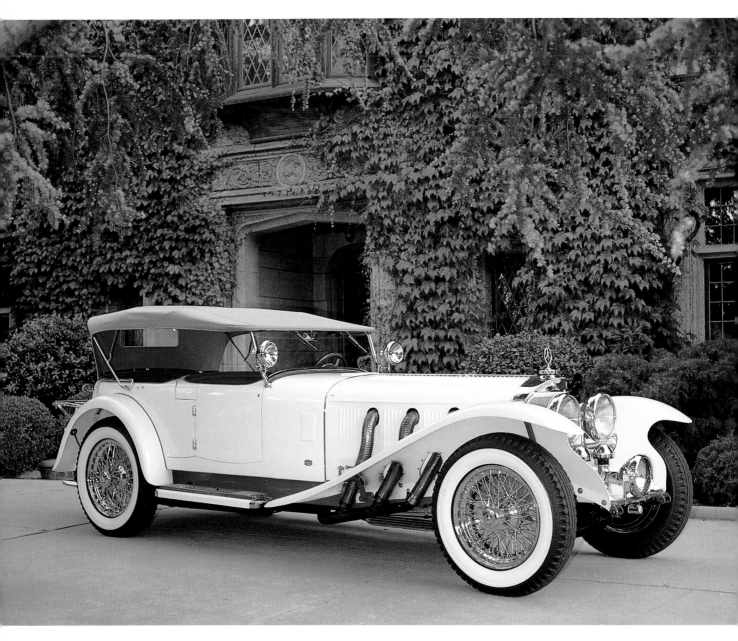

The Model S was built on a new drop-center frame with a 133in wheelbase. To improve the handling over the Model K, the new design moved the radiator and engine about a foot rearward on the chassis, resulting in better front–rear weight distribution and a lower center of gravity. This lower chassis also encouraged more rakish open coachwork on the Model S, such as the touring body pictured, designed by Gangloff and built by Zeitz in 1927. Styling for the Model S was more fashionable than any previous Benz or Mercedes model, and established new standards for design in the late 1920s.

In many ways, Mercedes-Benz, like so many great makes from the Classic Era, created visual icons that identified their cars regardless of coachwork. Grilles, of course, were obvious, but Mercedes interiors were also remarkably distinctive. Although instruments could be mounted in any number of configurations by a coachbuilder and in an equally varied selection of dashboard fascias—polished and engine-turned steel, wood veneers, or even leather—the massive, wood-rimmed Mercedes-Benz steering wheel was a true focal point of every SSK interior. It was unmistakable.

cars sold in America were treated to coachwork by the Walter M. Murphy Co. of Pasadena, California. The white SSK Boattail Speedster pictured is one of only two Mercedes chassis bodied by the American firm noted for its exemplary work on Duesenberg.

Perhaps the raciest looking SSK ever built, the Murphy Boattail was literally all hood and fenders, with the passenger compartment and Boattail deck barely extending beyond the radius of the rear wheels. The only other body style from this era that can even begin to rival the Murphy for the sheer impudence of its design is the famous SSK Sport-roadster built by Sindelfingen, with an equally exaggerated hood and impressive stack of spares mounted atop the rear deck.

Back in the 1920s, when people talked about motorcars, there were really two subjects to discuss: the coachwork (usually hand-fitted by one of several well-known coachbuilders or specially bodied by the factory) and the automobile's chassis (a separate structure that was for all intents the *real* automobile).

Nürburg 460

It was on the Mercedes-Benz stand, at the 1928 Olympia Motor Exhibition in London, that Daimler-Benz introduced the all-new 4.5ltr straight-eight Nürburg 460 model to Great Britain. The 460 chassis measured 12ft 1in in wheelbase with a narrow 4ft 9in track, and an overall length of 16ft 3in. Suspension was by semi-elliptic springs with Houdaille shock absorbers. The 460 offered four-wheel brakes with a vacuum servo system, automatic central chassis lubrication, and a choice of wooden or wire spoke wheels with Rudge hubs.

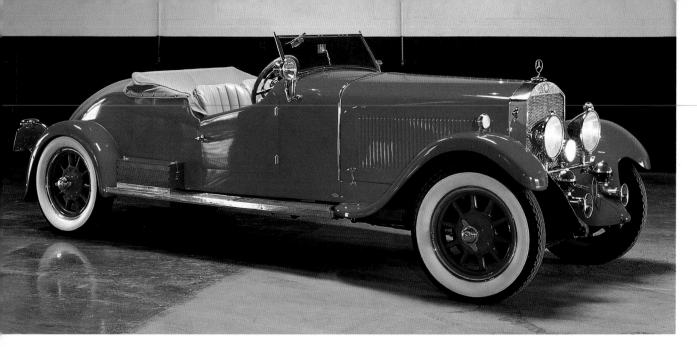

The right-hand-drive chassis beneath this car was one of the first produced in the new 1928 Nürburg series, named after the Nürburgring racing circuit where the car was tested. A pre-production prototype was wrung-out in a punishing thirteen-day, nonstop endurance run, covering a distance of 20,000km (12,500mi), while maintaining an average speed of 64km/h (40.5mph). The record-setting 311-hour trial virtually doubled the time and distance previously achieved by a factory stock car, after which Mercedes christened the car the 460 Nürburg.

Powered by a non-supercharged side-valve straight-eight engine displacing 4,592cc (80mmx115mm bore and stroke), the 460 motor developed 90hp at 3200rpm. The 460 Nürburgs were used in motor-sport competition above 3000ft elevations, where the thinner air caused the otherwise all-powerful supercharged SSKs to suffer significant power losses or simply stop running altogether.

Powered by a non-supercharged side-valve straight-eight engine displacing 4,592cc with 80mmx115mm bore and stroke, the 460 motor developed 90hp at 3200rpm (German specifications indicated 80hp while British sales literature indicated 90hp for the 460) taken aftward by a 4-speed transmission, available with a choice of two gearbox ratios.

The 460 Nürburg chassis (W 08 and 460 K) were manufactured through 1933, with a total production of 2,893. The pressed-steel, drop-frame platform was offered in two wheelbase lengths, the standard 3.670m (145in) model and a 3.43m (135in) *kurz* version. The 1928 and 1929 Type 460 models were primarily bodied as limousines, open tourers, or cabriolets, while a supercharged 460 K chassis was available with the same body choices plus a special sport-roadster version.

By the end of the 1920s and into the 1930s, Mercedes-Benz models took a commanding lead in engineering and technology, offering suspension, engine, and transmission designs that were to become the standard of the world by 1940. The greatest prewar achievements in Mercedes' history, however, were to come in the brief period from 1933 to 1939.

LEFT: Upholstered in tan leather and complemented with a mahogany floor, the 460 Nürburg Sport-Roadster takes on a far more elegant appearance than in racing trim.

BELOW: Dr. Ferdinand Porsche can be seen standing behind the number 6 on this 1922 Austro-Daimler race car, driven by Alfred Neubauer in the 1924 Targa Florio. Neubauer became head of the Daimler-Benz racing department and would be instrumental in the company's racing successes throughout the late 1930s and in the '50s. *Photo courtesy Mercedes-Benz North America*

CHAPTER FOUR

The 500K, 540K, and Cars of the 1930s:

The Kings of the Road

The magnificent coachwork created at Sindelfingen for the 500K and 540K is considered by many to be the most beautifully conceived of the classic era, and perhaps even of all time. Revered and valued today as true works of art, these classic portraits in steel conceal beneath their elaborate, hand-formed body panels yet another work of automotive art.

The 500K and 540K chassis represented the culmination of an era in which Daimler and Benz had merged their respective design and engineering talents to create the most influential and powerful automotive company in all of Europe. The chassis upon which Sindelfingen and nearly all of the great German, French, and British coachbuilders of the '30s left their mark were more than steelwork platforms upon which to attach a body.

The chassis design originated in 1933 with the short-lived Type 380. Only 154 were produced before the underpowered 3.8ltr motor housed beneath the imposing Sindelfingen coachwork was replaced by a new 5.0ltr straight-eight in 1934.

Although it would be difficult to refer to any 540K model as anything less than stunning, some were more so than others. The Special Coupe, rarity notwithstanding, was one of the most striking of all Sindelfingen designs because it managed, as no other 540K had, to blend the sweeping fenderlines and tapered rear deck of the sporty roadster with the refined elegance and style of a closed coupe—a feat attempted by numerous automakers throughout the 1930s but never executed as beautifully as on the 540K Special Coupes. *Fred Kriz collection.*

The 500K and 540K models measured 5.250m (206-3/4in), from bumper to bumper, on a 3.290m (129-1/2in) standard wheelbase chassis. Track measured 1.515m (59-5/8in) in front and 1.502m (59-1/8in) rear. The 500K and 540K chassis could also be ordered in a short K (*Kurz*) wheelbase of 2.98m (117.5 in). The chassis weight was 1,700kg (3,750lb). The radiator was a masterpiece of workmanship in itself. One of the most complex radiator designs of all time, its magnificent appearance was also the source of its greatest problems—maintenance and restoration! The interior of the radiator was formed with individually soldered tubes. The chromed shell was also more than decorative, it held the water.

The engineering of the chassis and its four-wheel independent suspension, pioneered by Daimler-Benz in the early 1930s, allowed unparalleled handling and comfort. Designed by Fritz Nallinger and his predecessor, Dr. Hans Nibel, the rear suspension used a swing-axle with two massive coil springs per side. The front suspension was comprised of parallel wishbones and one coil spring per side. To best take advantage of the engine's output, the cars were equipped with a 4-speed manual transmission, designed by Wilhelm Maybach. Despite their tremendous weight, the cars could accelerate from a stand to 62mph (100km/h) in only 16.5sec; another 14sec and the 500K was clocking 80mph. In top gear, it could attain a maximum speed of over 100mph; in the 1930s, any automobile that could achieve triple digits was immediately legendary.

The chassis was designed with the coachbuilder in mind, providing a platform that could be fitted with a wide variety of body styles, yet always retaining an appearance that one journalist in the 1930s described as having "aggressive styling and Teutonic arrogance."

The exhaust pipes, which have become a 540K hallmark, are contained inside the polished flex pipe heat shields. Looking at the chassis from the driver's perspective we see where the exhaust system goes through an oval cutout in the chassis frame rail. On the right side of the frame, a heat shield protected the wooden floorboard of the passenger compartment from the muffler. Here we also have an excellent view of the transmission housing. The 540K was equipped with a four-gang gearbox, designed by Wilhelm Maybach.

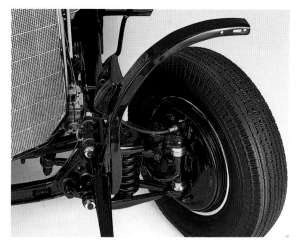

The independent front suspension was designed to absorb road vibrations and allow a more comfortable ride through the use of rubber mountings. The design also allowed the front wheels to flex slightly to the rear on impact with a bump, further absorbing vibrations before being taken up into the chassis. The double A-arm is clearly shown in this picture, along with the coil spring. The shock absorber is a lever-type carried on the outside behind the spring and attached from the chassis to the top A-arm.

Considered to be cars of uncommon quality, comfort and style, the 500Ks also proved their exceptional durability and strength in the *Deutschland Fahrt* (roughly "Tour of Germany") endurance tests in 1934. Covering a distance of 2,195.8km (approximately 1,364mi)—from Baden-Baden, through Stuttgart, Munich, Nuremberg, Dresden, Berlin (Avus), Magdeburg, Cologne, Nürburgring, and Mannheim, and back to Baden-Baden—the factory 500Ks, along with privately-owned Mercedes-Benz entries, virtually dominated a field of more than 190 vehicles.

With the addition of a 5.4ltr engine in 1936, the Mercedes reached its epitome. Producing 115hp standard, and a spirited 180hp with supercharger, this was one of the most powerful production automobiles in the world.

A total of 406 540K chassis were produced from 1936 through early 1940 (in addition there were 354 500K chassis built from 1934 to 1936).

Aside from a handful of custom-built bodies, Sindelfingen produced nearly all 500K and 540K coachwork, and in many more varieties than the usual Cabriolets and Special Roadsters we're accustomed to seeing at modern-day Concours d'Elegance.

According to Jan Melin's in-depth researching of factory records, there were over a dozen body types produced: the limousine, also called an Innenlenker or saloon; the formal Pullman-Limousine; the Spezial-Coupé; Kombinations-Coupé (a convertible coupe with optional removable hard top); the Autobahn-Kurier or Stromlinien-Limousine; a Normal-Roadster, sometimes referred to as Sport-Roadster; the Spezial-Roadster, distinguished by its concealed top, metal boot, and divided "V" windshield; Offener Tourenwagen "open tourer" or phaeton; and a series of cabriolets (A, B, C, D, and F, the latter two being exceptionally rare).

Although it would be difficult to refer to any 540K model as anything less than stunning, some

ABOVE: Fine, hand-sewn leather upholstery accented the 540K's interior. Instrument panel has mother-of-pearl inlays surrounding the instruments.

LEFT: The 1935 540K Cabriolet A shown is an example of a 500K body fitted to a new 540K engine. One of the true transitional cars, it was ordered as a 500K on June 25, 1935, through the Daimler-Benz distributor in Weimar-Thueringenin, but fitted with one of the first 5.4ltr engines when delivered on July 15, 1935, to the Vogel Publishing House in Poessneck-Thueringenin. It is one of thirteen documented 500Ks equipped with the new Daimler-Benz 5.4ltr straight-eight. Of those fitted with the 540K engine, only three, including the car pictured, are known to exist currently. *Frank Cherry collection.*

were more so than others. The Special Coupe was one of *the* most striking of all Sindelfingen designs because it managed as no other 540K design had to blend the sweeping fenderlines and tapered rear deck of the sportish Roadster with the refined elegance and style of a closed coupe, a feat attempted by numerous automakers throughout the 1930s, but never executed as beautifully as the Mercedes.

The Germans have always had their own, often unique interpretations of certain words, and the Special Roadster was one such case. A roadster, as defined by Daimler-Benz, was a car that had no padded headliner in the convertible top, which could either fold down very low or be completely concealed. Lowering the top on a typical Mercedes-Benz cabriolet left a stack of fabric, bows, and headliner high enough to obscure the rear view.

If the 540K was conceived for the purpose of making a statement, the Special Roadster was the last word. Introduced at the 1936 Berlin Auto Show, which coincided with the 50th anniversary of the Benz Patent-Motorwagen, the 540K Special Roadster was the most expensive Mercedes-Benz model offered that year.

What made the Special Roadster special? Paramount was its no-compromise styling. Passenger capacity of this huge car was four, two in the cockpit and two in the rumble seat. Extensive chromium embellishments were used along the fenders, hood, doors, and rear deck. These, and all of the chromed handles for doors, hood and rumble seat, required special castings.

LEFT: The 1935 Model 500K Special Sport Roadster pictured is one of the earliest of that body style built by the Sindelfingen factory. Approximately twelve of these true roadster bodies (those having side curtains rather than roll-up windows) were produced in 1935–36. Chassis number 123778, this car appears to be the sixth special roadster built, although the Komm.-Nr. 202124 would make it the third 500K model built. Such contradictions in records are not unusual.

Another unique feature was the sharply angled vee-windshield. Spotlights on either side of the windshield frame were also specially made for the car, each with a convex mirror attached to the back of its housing, serving as the only means of seeing alongside or to the rear.

If the 540K was conceived for the purpose of making a statement, the Special Roadster was the last word. Introduced at the 1936 Berlin Auto Show, which conveniently coincided with the fiftieth anniversary of the Benz Patent-Motorwagen, the 540K Special Roadster was the most expensive Mercedes-Benz model offered that year. The massive car allowed room for just two in the passenger compartment and a second couple in the rumble seat, if they dared. Interior was upholstered in fine hand-sewn leather and instruments were surrounded by a mother-of-pearl dashboard. *Jerry Sauls collection.*

Seating in the Special Roadster and Cabriolet A was intended for just two, although an occasional seat for one person could be fitted behind the front seats.

NEXT PAGE TOP RIGHT AND LEFT: The 540K interiors changed over the years. From the very elegant look of the 1937 dashboard with its fine jewel-like gauges (left), to the more contemporary look of this late-1939 model (one of the last built before the war) featuring an entirely new style of instruments and dash fascia and the addition of a dashboard-mounted radio.

BELOW: Coachwork for the 540K could vary from year to year. An excellent example is this 1937 Sport Cabriolet A, which combines styling cues more commonly associated with the Special Roadster, but with the more formal Cabriolet bars.

The 540K Special Roadster brought many firsts. It was the first Mercedes-Benz to be dressed in silver metallic paint, known to Daimler-Benz as "fisch-silver grau," and was the first to enjoy a completely disappearing convertible top, stowed beneath a metal lid. The interior was also atypical, highlighted by a steering wheel, gearshift knob, emergency brake han-

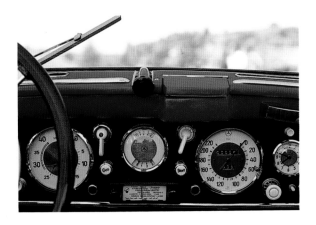

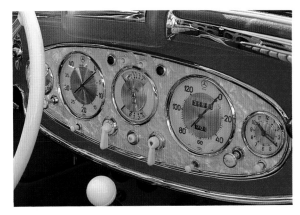

dle, and reserve fuel knob all in white. Instruments of watch-like quality were usually surrounded by a mother-of-pearl dashboard fascia, adding the final touch of elegance to the car's interior.

290

Not every great car built by Daimler-Benz in the 1930s was a 500K or a 540K. Few were, in fact. The lesser series, such as the 290, were far more important to the company's survival. With an inline 6-cylinder engine, the 290 was never intended to be as flamboyant as the more costly 8-cylinder 500K and 540K, yet they were often fitted with exceptional coachwork. The 290 was an evolutionary model, incorporating advanced designs, such as a dropped box-section frame with four-wheel fully independent suspension, overdrive gearbox, divided track-rod steering, hydraulic brakes, and one-shot lubrication.

While readily available to a large segment of the market, the 290 became a *bijou* version of the 540K for many buyers. Most 290 bodies were traditional and rather ordinary, distinguished mainly by the Mercedes-Benz grille and star. The few exceptions were the Streamlined Saloon, Roadster, and Cabriolet. One book on Mercedes-Benz catalogs twenty-five different body styles on the 290's 2.88m (113in) short chassis and 3.3m (130in) long chassis.

While nearly all of the 290s built were assembled at the Mannheim Werke and bore the Mannheim emblem just forward of the driver's door, a number were bodied by the Sindelfingen Werke. The average price of a luxury 290 model was exactly half that of a 540K.

170

The total number of 290s built between 1933 and 1937 was just 8,214. Hardly mass production. In comparison, Mercedes-Benz turned out more than 39,000 of the popular and less expensive 170 and 170V models during the same period.

In the 1930s, the best-selling car to wear a Mercedes-Benz star was the 170, and of all the low cost models offered, the sporty 170V Roadster was the consummate example. With the top stowed neatly out of sight behind the front seats, and the shifter finally snicked into high gear, it was one of the most enjoyable and affordable cars in Mercedes-Benz history. In 1938, if you had roughly $1,250 to spend on a new automobile, you could have purchased a 170V Roadster.

Cars like the 170V were the bread-and-butter models. A total of ten catalogued body styles were offered from 1936 through 1942, with production totaling nearly 100,000 units before the war ended commercial automobile manufacturing.

The original 170 models were introduced in 1931, as inexpensive cars whose very design and smaller engine displacement were mandated by the economic tide that had swept through Europe following the Depression. Intended as a conservative offering, the 170 nonetheless blazed some technological trails, offering features not available from other European car companies. For a base price of $1,000 in 1936, the car came with a responsive 1.7ltr 6-cylinder engine, four-wheel fully independent suspension, central lubrication, four-wheel hydraulic brakes, pressed steel wheels, and an anti-theft steering-wheel lock. While any one of these features might have been found on competitive auto-

The 290 models were more affordable than the 540K—about half the price—yet very stylish. According to the German specifications for the Type 290 W18, the 6-cylinder engine displaced 2,867cc with a bore and stroke of 78x100mm and an output of 68hp. This example has a custom body styled after the 540K Cabriolets.

mobiles, no other European car of that day offered all of them at anything like the 170's price.

Although they sold well, early 170s lacked, somewhat, in eye appeal. Even the lines of its sporty two-seat Roadster were square and stodgy. In 1936, the 170V gave the model line a new, more daring appearance.

To improve structural design and ride quality, a new tubular backbone frame replaced the original box-section chassis used on the 170. The V was also noticeably longer than its predecessor, riding on a 2.845m (113.8in) wheelbase versus the 170's 2.600m (104in) platform.

Another intermediate model was the type 230. This model was equipped with a 6-cylinder engine developing 55hp. Body styles also were similar to the more costly 540K. Cabriolet A models were produced in 1936 and '37. *Jerry J. Moore collection.*

The greatest change, however, lay beneath the hood, where a more efficient 4-cylinder engine replaced the 170's 6-cylinder motor. In comparison, the 170V displaced 1,697cc, with a bore and stroke of 73.5x100mm and output of 38hp at 3,400rpm versus the six's 1,692cc displacement, 65x85mm bore and stroke, and 32hp. Top speed was improved as well from a maximum of 90km/h (56mph) to 108km/h (67mph). A new 4-speed transmission completed the mechanical revisions.

More than a high-water mark for Mercedes-Benz popularity, the 170V was also the foundation for the company's revival after WWII. The compact 4-cylinder sedan was the first postwar Mercedes-Benz produced. Regrettably, nothing remotely like the sporty 170V rumble-seat Roadster would appear again.

CHAPTER FIVE

The Era of Reconstruction:

Mercedes-Benz in the Late 1940s and Early 1950s

I n America, owning a Mercedes-Benz has become a symbol of success, but would you feel as regal behind the wheel of your new C220 or its 190 predecessor if you knew that in Germany they are used as airport taxi cabs? Daimler-Benz has been manufacturing commercial vehicles since the 1920s.

Despite a product line as diversified as that of General Motors, Mercedes-Benz is best known for having built the most expensive cars of all time. Indeed, Mercedes-Benz built the *voiture* of choice for German aristocracy and European gentry, but they were *not* the cars that paid the bills. This job was left to the Mercedes-Benz 170, the Mercedes for the masses.

Model 170

In the late 1930s, the 170s had been offered with only a 4-cylinder gas engine. By 1945 nearly all of DBAG's factories had been leveled to the ground, and the 170V was one of the few cars for which tooling remained intact.

The Type 220S, manufactured from the mid-50s through 1960, was the conduit through which this bygone era would pass, leaving behind it an image that would not easily be forgotten. The 220S, "S" for super, was introduced in 1956, the third of three new models making their public debut at the Frankfurt Auto Show. Two years into 220S production, a fuel-injected six was introduced and cars so equipped were designated 220SE. Introduced in September 1958, production continued through November 1960. The SE Coupe and S Cabriolet pictured are from the Al Douglas Collection. The 220s represented the new contemporary look of Mercedes-Benz.

The postwar reconstruction of Daimler-Benz AG was quite literally built on the back of the 170V, about the only car for which tooling remained intact. The first postwar production cars were introduced in 1947 and were, for all intents, 1942 models. Within two years the rebuilt assembly lines were producing 170 models equipped with either a 4-cylinder gasoline engine or a new 1.7ltr pushrod-ohv diesel developing 38hp at 3200rpm. *Photo courtesy Mercedes-Benz North America*

The first postwar production cars were introduced in 1947 and were, for all intents, 1942 models. Within two years rebuilt assembly lines were producing 170 models equipped with either a 4-cylinder gasoline engine or a new 1.7ltr, pushrod ohv diesel. Daimler-Benz had been offering diesel engines as an option on specific models since 1936, when the German automaker introduced the world's first diesel passenger car, the 2.5ltr 260D.

An improved Type 170Da was introduced in May of 1950 with production running through April 1952. The 170Da was slightly more powerful, having a larger displacement of 1.77ltr and an output of 40hp (DIN). The 170Da was followed by the 170Db model, featuring a wider track, hypoid rear axle, a slightly revised hoodline, and a larger windshield. They were produced until October 1953.

The final series, beginning with the 170DS, was built concurrently with the 170Da and 170Db, from January 1952 until August 1953. The very last version, the 170S-D, was produced from July 1953 until September 1955 when the entire 170 model line was retired, as were their old prewar body styles. From the first to the last postwar 170 models, a total of 153,475 were built, yet few can be found today.

If there was one significant factor separating American cars built in the early 1950s from those produced in Europe during the same period, it was styling. Designers in America were experimenting with new ideas, trying to break away from the dated '40s look that had seemingly been held in a state of suspended animation by the war years. Throughout much of Europe the battlefield had extended right up to the front door of the world's oldest and most

Though not particularly fast, the 170 Diesel's torque curve was very steady, applying power over a wide range of engine speeds, giving the car a maximum speed of 62mph in top gear. In 1949, Britain's automotive journal *The Autocar*, reviewed the 170D stating that, "On the road the car gave a pleasant ride, being slightly slower than with the comparable petrol engine, but the performance on winding, hilly roads left little to be desired. The engine was reasonably silent, chiefly owing to the large rubber mountings which also absorb a considerable proportion of the vibrations. The [car's] four-wheel independent suspension gave excellent road-holding, even over bad paved roads, with a full complement of passengers." *Walter Worsch collection*

established automakers, leaving them little choice but to pick up the pieces of a broken industry and begin building cars whose designs were cemented in the past. A blessing if you will, to those who appreciate the sheer beauty of British, Italian, and German cars produced in the early postwar 1940s and '50s.

300 Series

The Type 300 and companion 220 series were the first Daimler-Benz models to introduce entirely new postwar styling, with a more streamlined, envelope-type body incorporating the headlamps into the front fenders. The 300 was also the first Mercedes designed with an eye to the American

The 300 was succeeded by the 300b, built from March 1954 until August 1955. The 300b offered the same body equipped with front vent windows, larger brakes, revised gearing, and a more powerful 125hp M186II engine, achieved through a higher compression ratio—7.4 or 7.5:1—and either Solex 32 PAITA or PAIAT two-barrel carburetors. The car pictured is a 300b, built in 1953. The b-models used the typical Mercedes-Benz four-wheel independent suspension, providing the large sedans and convertibles with an exceptionally smooth ride and responsive handling.

market, a market 20 million deep, and clamoring for anything new.

Coachwork for the Type 300 was produced at the Daimler-Benz factory in Sindelfingen. Available in only two body styles, a slim-pillar, four-door sedan and a pillarless four-door convertible, the 300 series looked modern, yet quintessentially German. Daimler-Benz AG's general director, Dr. Wilhelm Haspel, had instructed body engineer Karl Wilfert and his staff to ensure that Mercedes' traditional, upright radiator motif would be an integral part of the all-new 300-series design. In an automotive era when "all-new" often meant the elimination of tradition, that decision was pivotal and has not since been violated.

Current styling director Bruno Sacco, who joined Mercedes-Benz in 1958, describes the 300-series Sedan as the "high-status German car of the 1950s." The 300 Sedan was the choice of embassies, dignitaries, and heads of state. In Germany, it was often referred to as the *"Adenauer-Wagen,"* after West German Chancellor Konrad Adenauer, one of many prominent political figures who chose the 300 for personal transportation. Properly referred to in Germany as a *Limousine 4 Türen*, Sacco wrote of the 300 series, "This design concept was ultra-conservative, obviously with an eye on Rolls-Royce. Remember, we're discussing 1951. When you consider that this car concept was continually being improved and rolled off the assembly lines in Sindelfingen until 1962, you will conclude that the clientele was happy with it. However, that clientele was a major risk for the survival of the company; it was dying out."

In its overall design, the Type 300 was a tremendously impressive car, particularly the four-door convertible sedan. In America, the 300 was virtually in a class by itself, with the possible exception of the early postwar Packard Clippers. Both had the same sweeping front fenders fading into the front doors, a long, graceful hoodline, and a tall, distinctive radiator shell.

One of the longest running models in the company's history, the 300 series had an 11-year production life. The first-series sedan was built from late 1951 through March 1954, with regular production of the four-door convertible beginning in April 1952.

The original 300 models were succeeded by the 300b, externally unchanged, but delivering 10 more horsepower and equipped with larger brakes. Although popular, production figures were never

The 300b was powered by a 6-cylinder engine displacing 3.0ltr (182.8ci) with an almost square bore and stroke of 85x88mm (3.35x3.46in). Compression ratio was 6.4:1, and the engine developed a substantial 115hp at 4600rpm. The 120in wheelbase sedan weighed 3,895lb, and in top gear could attain a speed of 96mph. The ohc six used in the 300 evolved into the later M198 engine used in the first 300SL sports cars.

high, around 6,200 sedans and a scant 591 convertibles in both series, through the summer of 1955.

The 300c, introduced in September 1955, ran through June 1956. Altogether, Daimler-Benz produced only 1,430 of the 300c Sedans and fifty-one Convertibles. The last in the series, the 300d were built on a longer 124in wheelbase (versus the original 120in platform). The body was updated with a flatter, more squared-up roofline, longer rear fenders, and a slightly wider grille. And, in keeping with contemporary styling, the d-series sedan lost its fixed center pillars to become a four-door hardtop. Mechanical fuel injection from the 300Sc and SL was also adopted, along with a higher compression ratio, increasing output to 160hp. Offered from late 1957 through early 1962, the 300d saw production of nearly 3,100 hardtops and sixty-five convertibles.

Although the 300 series may not have been great in numbers, with a total production of only 11,430 cars over an 11-year period, the real value was in rebuilding the luxury image Mercedes-Benz had established in the 1920s and '30s. This, the Type 300 accomplished in a fashion few other automobiles have ever managed!

One can only marvel at the Mercedes-Benz 300S and Sc, cars that evoked the same emotion that had

ABOVE: A 1955 300c Sedan sold for DM 23,500, approximately $7,000; it was often chosen by foreign embassies for its long wheelbase and large, comfortable interior. The option list included possibly the largest sunroof ever built. The manually operated Webasto fabric top moved along narrow tracks, folding over itself ever so neatly on the way back, to expose the entire front and rear passenger compartments. Similar sunroof designs date back to the 1920s, both in Europe and America, but few cars have used a folding sunroof on as grand a scale as the 300c.

LEFT: There was never a problem fitting your luggage into the 300Sc's steeply angled trunk. Every 300S and Sc came with its own custom leather luggage set.

The 300Sc, which appeared late in 1955 as a '56 model, introduced sweeping changes, proof that Daimler-Benz was constantly improving its cars, even if they were only going to build 200 of them! The 3.0ltr ohc 6-cylinder engine was now Bosch fuel-injected and closely related to the 300SL's. The Sc developed 175hp at 5400rpm, bettering the S by 25 horses from the same 182.7ci displacement. *Ned Tannen collection.*

been stirred men's souls a score of years before by the great Mercedes 540K. The 300S was a perfect combination of hand-crafted Old World coachwork and classically inspired bodylines blended with a contemporary chassis, suspension, and driveline.

Introduced in October 1951 at the Paris Auto Salon, the 300S was by design an overtly sporting car, the first such model to come from Stuttgart since the end of World War II. In little more than five years' time, Mercedes-Benz had gone from near ruin, to producing automobiles that were once again the envy of motoring cognoscente the world over.

Virtually hand-built to order, the S and Sc were far more expensive than any other Mercedes-Benz 300 models, the Sc demanding over $12,500, nearly twice

that of the sporty Gullwing Coupe, and more than almost any other automobile sold in America.

After two years, the 300S was updated to the 300Sb version with the addition of finned brake drums, vent windows, improved heating, and a Becker Mexico in place of a Becker Nürburg radio. The 300Sc, which appeared late in 1955 as a '56 model, introduced sweeping changes, proof that Daimler-Benz was constantly improving its cars, even if they were only going to build 200 of them! The 3.0ltr ohc 6-cylinder engine was now fuel-injected (*Einspritzmotor*) and closely related to the 300SL's, utilizing a Bosch injection pump. With a compression ratio increased from 7.8:1 to 8.55:1, the Sc developed 175hp at 5400rpm, bettering the S by 25 horses from the same

Mercedes' new 220 models, equipped with a 2.2ltr 6-cylinder engine, were first shown in April 1951. A contemporary of the larger 300S, the 220 was among the last models to sport prewar-inspired coachwork. The 220 was manufactured in three body styles: Sedan and

Cabriolets A and B. A variation of the Cabriolet A, known as a Cabriolet Coupe (pictured) was fitted with a hardtop. Only eighty-five were built for the 1954 and '55 model years. Total production for the 220 model line reached 18,514.

The rights of passage were performed for Daimler-Benz by the 300Sc and 220SE models. The 300Sc was the last "classically-inspired" design to come from the Sindelfingen *werke*. The design of the modern 220SE clearly departed from all past styling cues traditional to Daimler-Benz, save for the upright grille and three-pointed star hood ornament. The most advanced of the round-body models, the 220SE was virtually identical to the 220S, but its intermittent mechanical fuel injection and a different camshaft gave the engine 130hp. *Jerry J. Moore collection.*

182.7ci displacement. The drive was taken to the rear through a fully synchronized 4-speed manual transmission, with either a standard column or sportier floor-mounted shift. Mercedes-Benz literature of 1956 claimed 200hp from the Sc engine, with a top speed of 112mph. Despite a curb weight of up to 4,450lb, the Sc could deliver its occupants from 0 to 60mph in a respectable 14sec.

Comfort and performance were given greater consideration in the Sc, which introduced a new and more responsive independent rear suspension, utilizing a single low-pivot point rear swing axle with coil springs. (The single-pivot design was adapted the following year for the 1957 300SL Roadster.)

Aside from the engine changes and the use of larger brake drums to pull the Sc's down from speed, the 300S and Sc shared the same specifications of design and were available in similar models: cabriolet, coupe and roadster. All three body styles had a wheelbase of 114.2in, an overall length of 185in, and a front and rear track measuring 58.2 and 60in, respectively.

Interior appointments of the 300S and Sc were done in the same fashion as in prewar Mercedes-Benz cars, with plush, roll-and-pleat leather upholstery and fine wood veneers in the buyer's choice of burled or straight-grain walnut, lacquered to a glass-like finish. There was never a problem fitting your luggage into the car's steeply angled trunk; every 300S and Sc came with its own custom leather luggage set designed for the trunk.

For the 1950s, the 300Sc offered features precious few automakers even had on their drawing boards: four-wheel, fully-independent suspension and ventilated, bi-metal, vacuum-assisted brakes, along with a number of safety and convenience features such as backup lights, turn signals, non-glare mirrors, and windshield washers. Inside were reclining seats, a signal-seeking radio, and appointments that today are still considered luxury options. A total of just 760 cars were built from 1952 to 1958.

220 Series

The 1950s were a time of change, a time to let go of old ideas and embrace new ones. In 1953 the new 180 Sedan brought unit-body construction and contemporary 1950s styling to Mercedes-Benz for the first time. To Daimler-Benz AG's conservative management, this car represented such a bold step that they continued to offer the old prewar-styled 170 and 220, just in case the all-new 180 should prove to be unpopular. It did not. The following year a new 6-cylinder model, the 220a, was introduced. Also of unit-body construction and similar in design to the 180, it started a new 6-cylinder dynasty.

The 220S ("S" for "Super") came along in 1956, the third of three new models making their debut at the Frankfurt Auto Show. Along with the new 190 and 219, the 220S, most powerful and most expensive of the trio, represented Daimler-Benz's new contemporary look, bidding a final farewell to the vestigial fender lines of the classic 1930s and '40s. The styling was integrated, fenders and body sides forming one plane, seasoned perhaps with a hint of classic lineage in its rear quarter treatment.

The new 220S four-door sedans sold well, but Daimler-Benz knew that it could be transformed into a coupe or convertible that would attract the buyer who wanted a more exclusive model. The sedan's 111in wheelbase was cut to 106.3in for the coupe and convertible, which measured 183.9in in overall length to the sedan's 187in.

The M180 2,195cc (133.9ci) sohc 6-cylinder engine was used in the same basic form in the 219, but with dual Solex carburetors which allowed it to develop 112hp, 20 more than the 219 with its single carburetor. Bore and stroke were (3.15x2.86in), and compression ratio was 7.6:1. After August 1957 this was boosted to 8.7:1, increasing peak power to 124hp for the 220S and 100hp for the 219.

In September 1958, two years into 220S production, the fuel-injected 220SE version was introduced. The most advanced of the round-body models, the 220SE was virtually identical with the exception of its intermittent mechanical fuel injection and a different camshaft. Horsepower increased to 130, torque went up by 5 percent, and fuel efficiency was improved by 8 percent.

With the introduction of the new 220Sb finback sedans, the round-body 220SE sedans were discontinued, though the coupe and convertible 220SEs remained in production, overlapping that of the new 220SEb sedan until November 1960.

The first full decade of the postwar era had seen Mercedes-Benz return to prominence in both luxury and sports car design and manufacturing, a feat hardly anyone but Mercedes-Benz would have thought possible.

CHAPTER SIX

The World's Best Sports Car:

Mercedes-Benz 300SL

On February 6, 1954, Daimler-Benz introduced the 300SL Coupe to the world at New York's International Motor Sports Show. Something of a milestone, this was the first time Mercedes-Benz had ever shown a new model in the United States before it was introduced in Germany.

At the time of its unveiling, the 300SL took everyone by surprise. The aggressive styling of Italian and British sports cars, however appealing, appeared almost antiquated alongside the dramatic shape of the 300SL, a luxurious adaptation of the triumphant 1952 Mercedes-Benz 300SL race cars.

The 300SL engine (as with the 1952 race car engines), was a direct adaptation of the sohc six used in the 300-series Sedan, Coupe, Cabriolet, and Roadster. Although the competition cars had used three Solex 40 PBJC down-draft carburetors and twin electric fuel pumps, the 3.0ltr engines for the production models received fuel through direct mechanical injection, the first such application of this system in a series production, gasoline-powered automobile.

The maximum 215hp (240hp with the sports camshaft) arrived at the rear wheels via a 4-speed synchromesh gearbox and a ZF limited-slip differential. At peak performance the production 300SL could attain 150mph and reach 60mph from rest in 8sec. For privateer competition, the cars could be ordered with

The 300SL Gullwing has become the most famous '50s-era sports car in the world. Regarded as the ultimate postwar collectible sports car, the Gullwing is rarely overshadowed, except by the occasional rare Ferrari model.

ABOVE AND RIGHT: The sleek, rounded contours of the 300SL body were a perfect match for Uhlenhaut's tubular space frame. Slipping through the air, the cars carried no superfluous trim, no door handles—nothing to increase wind resistance. The wind tunnel revealed a drag coefficient of 0.29, a figure that car manufacturers find challenging more than forty years later! *Drawing courtesy Mercedes-Benz North America*

a 4.11:1 rear axle ratio (designed for hill climbs or short American road courses) or a choice of either 3.89:1, 3.64:1 (the most common on Gullwings in the United States), 3.42:1 (geared for higher top speeds), or the 3.25:1 (which allowed the highest maximum speed). With the 3.25:1 rear axle the terminal velocity (as tested by Daimler-Benz) was a remarkable 161.5mph. Realistically, the cars could easily reach 150mph, making them the fastest production automobiles available in the 1950s.

In addition to the standard Gullwings, a limited run of twenty-nine all-aluminum 300SLs were built in 1955 and '56. As a matter of record, *all* 300SL Coupes had aluminum hoods, trunk lids, rocker panels, firewall, seat tub, and doors. The rest of the body was steel. The lighter alloy cars were custom built at the factory as special orders and were additionally fitted with plexiglass windows and back lights to further reduce weight. (The windshields were still glass.) The standard production Coupe weighed 2,849lb dry, and the alloy cars weighed 2,669lb.

Designers Karl Wilfert and Paul Bracq had done an incredible job of turning a purpose-built race car into a civilized, road-going sports car, and in less than a year's time. However, underneath Wilfert's more streamlined bodywork and luxuriously appointed in-

In addition to the 300SL Coupe, Mercedes-Benz introduced the 300SL Roadster in 1957, which replaced the Gullwing that same year. Roadsters were also available with a removable hardtop. Some 1,858 Roadsters were built from '57 through 1964.

terior, the 300SL had changed little from the original 1952 competition coupes. Air conditioning was not available, ventilation was minimal, and entry and exit was over the wide elbow-high door sill. Luggage was restricted to a bag or two in the trunk and what could be packed in the optional two-piece luggage set.

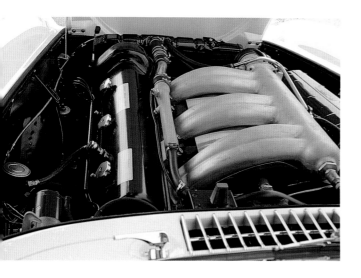

LEFT: The powerful M198 fuel-injected 6-cylinder engine used in the 300SL delivered 240hp at 5800rpm with the sports camshaft.

BELOW: Contrary to popular belief, planning for the 300SL Roadster began before the first production coupes were even delivered. Archive documents indicate that design and construction was to take place beginning in October 1954 with the first roadster prototype being completed for evaluation by top management in November 1955. The designers of the Gullwing were well aware of its shortcomings from the beginning: no real luggage or trunk area, difficult handling due to the high-pivot rear axle, and difficult entry and exit due to the high door sills. The new Roadster would solve these problems. Additionally, the designers felt an open-model sports car would prove more popular in places like Southern California where 300SL sales were expected to be strong.
Photo courtesy Mercedes-Benz North America

The SL's very firm bucket seats gave excellent support and were offered in either Gaberdine plaid with tex-leather (vinyl), or hand-sewn leather throughout; the wide door sills created a perfect armrest. The majority of early cars came standard with fabric seats. Luggage was optional. All-around visibility was excellent, and thanks to the high fenders, drivers found it easy to get a feel for the car's length and width. After a few minutes behind the wheel, the 300SL seemed as familiar as a well-worn pair of driving gloves.

From behind the wheel, the driver had a clear view of the instrument panel which housed the tachometer (reading up to 8000rpm) on the left and speedometer (reading up to 160mph) on the right. Two warning lights were also located in the upper part of the dashboard—one for the high beam (blue) at the top, one for the turning indicators (yellow) further down. Two small gauges were located to the left of the steering wheel—fuel gauge and oil pressure—and to the right, another pair—oil and water temperature. Prominently displayed in the center of the dashboard was a clock. In the lower section of the panel a series of chrome-plated switches to operate the lights, windshield wipers, and heating and ventilation systems were arranged within easy reach of the driver.

Additionally, unless one had the skills of Stirling Moss, driving the 300SL properly and effectively was no easy task.

The 300SL Coupes were built through early 1957, and total production came to just 1,400. Of that, 146 were manufactured in 1954 with approximately 125 cars being sold in the United States that year. Of the entire production run, roughly 1,000 coupes found their way to America. Few enough and great enough to have earned the Gullwing a permanent niche in the pantheon of great sports cars.

The Gullwing was succeeded in 1957 by the 300SL Roadster. Introduced at the Geneva Motor Show, Daimler-Benz proudly stated that "the 300 SL Roadster is our response to the demand in many countries for a particularly fast, comfortable, open sports car. This automobile offers a wide range of technical achievements for even greater driving safety and motoring comfort as well as a high standard of practical everyday value for touring in real style."

Though not as competitive as the coupe, the roadster was the more comfortable and practical of the two 300SL models. The convertible top folded easily and conveniently beneath a hard boot that fit flush with the body, and a removable hardtop was also available as an option, giving the car a more distinctive look and added protection in winter. Mechanically it had a slightly more powerful engine and a revised rear suspension to improve handling. A bold, new, vertical headlamp design and a revised instrument panel layout added to the differentiation between the coupe and roadster. Beginning in 1961, roadsters were fitted with Dunlop's new disc brakes, bringing the final evolution of the 300SL to a conclusion, and with it the end of a chapter in automotive history. The legacy of the 300SL is that it will never be forgotten.

The 300SL Roadster was fitted with an entirely new dashboard and instrument panel design. As to which proved better, the Coupe's or the Roadster's, it has become a matter of personal taste. The Coupe featured twin round instruments; the Roadster featured round dials and new column-style gauges between.

CHAPTER SEVEN

The New Mercedes-Benz:

Cars of the 1960s

Progress. Indeed, we all want it, and every consumer-oriented business tries to give it to us. The trouble is, progress often takes a few steps to reach full maturity, and a lot of us stumble over those steps on the way to tomorrow's sweet promise.

For Daimler and Benz, progress in the design and development of the automobile was seldom a problem. After all, they invented it! In the 1920s Daimler and Benz, both individually and together, set the standards for the world with cars such as the 200hp Blitzen Benz and staggering 300hp SSKL. In the '30s, before anyone else had even seriously considered it, they were building automobiles with fully independent suspensions; and when the rest of the automotive world was producing boxy postwar sedans, stodgy coupes, and luxury cars with enough chrome to increase the gross national product of Rhodesia, Daimler-Benz was introducing the sleek, aerodynamic 300SL, a car almost devoid of chrome.

220SE

In February 1961, some 35 years after the two oldest and largest automobile companies in Germany merged to form Daimler-Benz AG, the 75th

Designed by Paul Bracq, who later penned the BMW Turbo prototype that evolved into the BMW M1, the 230SL incorporated a number of advanced styling and construction techniques. The car's most controversial feature was the "pagoda" roof, a design that was highly criticized for its odd shape but lauded for its unrivaled visibility and the "illusion of lightness" it provided the interior. *John Linden collection*

The 220SE's name was derived from the displacement of the engine, 2.2ltr, multiplied by 100, the "S" indicating that this car was senior to the firm's lower-priced models (just as S-Class Mercedes are distinguished today), and the "E" denoting *Einspritzung,* or fuel injection. The 220SEb introduced new body styling, breaking once and for all from the classically inspired lines of the 1958–60 220SE Coupe and Cabriolet models. In 1961, Daimler-Benz produced a total of 2,537 220SEb models. Total 220SEb production from September 1960 through October 1965 amounted to 16,902. *Bob Scudder collection*

Anniversary of the Patent-Motorwagen was celebrated with the opening of the new Daimler-Benz Automotive Museum in Stuttgart, and the public introduction of a new model, the Mercedes-Benz 220SE Coupe.

    The all-new 220SEb, also referred to as "the Jubilee Year Mercedes," differed greatly from the 220SE Coupe it replaced in 1961. It was a handsome, prestigious version of the 220SE Sedan, with two doors, four seats, and a sleek new body—the synthesis of a sports car and a touring car. A fuel-injected, 134hp 2.2ltr ohc 6-cylinder engine and floor-mounted 4-speed shifter provided sports-car-like performance, in contrast to the luxurious interior, finished with leather upholstery and fine hand-crafted wood veneer accents—the kind of sports coupe automakers build *today* because it's trendy. In 1961, it was trend setting.

    Although built in the same fashion as the previous 220 models, with unitized body construction, single joint

LEFT: To the rear, the 220SEb's fenderlines were absent of the "fins" introduced on 1959 220b sedans. The SEb Coupe and Cabriolet that followed were the epitome of Daimler-Benz styling—a look that would go almost unchanged for nearly a decade.

BELOW: The 220SE is a rare postwar model in any form, the 2/2 Coupe with sunroof even more so. Mercedes produced a total of 3,916 SEs from 1958 to 1960—1,974 sedans, 1,112 convertibles, and only 830 Coupes. List price for the Coupe with the semi-automatic transmission, sunroof, and radio was almost $9,000. Pretty expensive for 1960, especially when one could purchase a brand new top-of-the-line Cadillac Sixty Special for $6,223!

While the 220SE Convertible and Coupe were considered only mid-range luxury cars compared to the 300Sc, they were far from austere, with beautifully polished wood dashboards and door trim, chrome surrounds for the instruments and controls, and plush leather upholstery throughout. Continuing the winning style of the earlier 220, but in even more graceful proportions, the 220SE's have all been certified as Milestone cars, making these rare postwar Mercedes-Benz models true collectibles.

low-pivot swing axle independent rear and traditional Mercedes independent front suspension, the new SEb Coupe and Cabriolet rested on a 2-1/2in longer wheelbase (108.25in), and were 8in greater in overall length (192.5in), some 3in wider (72.7in), and 3in lower (56.1in).

Mechanically, the new SEb was the first Mercedes model to offer front disc brakes. In most other respects, it was unchanged from its predecessor, powered by a 2.2ltr six with Bosch intermittent induction-manifold injection, and an output of 134hp at 5000rpm, providing both the coupe and cabriolet with true sports acceleration right up to their maximum speed of 105mph.

Bruno Sacco, Daimler-Benz's director of design since 1986, joined the Daimler-Benz design staff early in 1958, when the 220SEb was on the drawing board. Says Sacco of the '61 coupe, "[It] is one of the most beautiful Mercedes ever designed, but not only that: it is one of the most beautiful cars ever designed anywhere. The proportions are just right, and there are no transient styling elements except for the buffers attached to the four corners of the vehicle."

RIGHT: One of the most interesting looking engine compartments of any Mercedes-Benz models, the 220SEb was powered by a 2.2ltr six with Bosch intermittent induction-manifold injection and an output of 134hp at 5000rpm. Maximum speed was 105mph.

The 230, 250, and 280SLs were discovered not only by women, but also by doctors, lawyers, entertainers, and corporate executives, all of whom wanted a sports car without sports-car compromises. The new SLs gave them this and more: power steering, air conditioning, and if shifting gears was deemed a burden, even automatic transmission.

In his 1988 book, *Mercedes-Benz Design*, Sacco wrote, "The vertically arranged headlight unit, introduced with the 300SL Roadster, reached its height with the 220SEb. Also of particular interest, was the horizontal arrangement of the very large rear light unit." A styling cue that has since become a constant in Mercedes-Benz design.

While the merits of any automotive design are purely subjective—what plays well in Stuttgart might be received less charitably in Des Moines—few will argue that the 220SEb Coupe was as near perfect a blend of form and function as any automaker in the early '60s achieved.

230SL, 250SL, and 280SL

For Mercedes-Benz, introducing a car to *replace* the 300SL wasn't possible. Chief Engineer Rudolf Uhlenhaut set out to design a car that would combine the best characteristics of both the 300SL and the less expensive 190SL. This amalgamation, together with all new styling and improved handling, brought forth a remarkable generation of Mercedes-Benz SL models for the 1960s.

On its own, the 230SL and later 250 and 280 variants were consummate examples of Mercedes-Benz design and engineering. Although these were cars that had been well thought out, in the eyes of many sports car cognoscenti still smitten with the 300SL they were not a suitable replacement. The 230SL came not only on the heels of the 300 but at the same time as Jaguar's XK-E and the Corvette Stingray, two cars that were undeniably more exotic in appearance.

The 230SL had a difficult mission, to bridge the distance between pure *race-bred* sports car design and a more civilized, more contemporary road car. Introduced in March 1963 at the Geneva Auto Show, the new Mercedes was more than it appeared to be, but less than anyone had expected. Where once had been a sleek, curvaceous roadster now stood a boxy two-seater powered by a sohc 2.3ltr 6-cylinder engine developing only 150hp. Despite the fact that the car had better handling, vastly improved comfort, and a higher level of options, nay-sayers were hard-pressed to call it a "sports car." Mercedes-Benz wasted little time in proving the SL's mettle, entering a virtually stock 230SL in the grueling Spa–Sofia–Liege rally—the European

equivalent of the Baja 1000 for sheer abuse to driver and machine. Mercedes-Benz came away with a decisive victory. There was no doubt that this car was cut from the same cloth as the great 300SL.

The 230SL took a new direction from other two-passenger sports cars of the period. Built on a comparatively short 94.5in wheelbase, the car had a wide track, 58.3in front and 58.5in rear. The 230SL's stance was some 8in wider than that of the Jaguar XK-E. The result was exceptionally well-mannered and predictable handling.

As had been its practice since the early 1930s, Mercedes-Benz sports cars rode on a four-wheel fully independent suspension. The 230SL used an advanced low-pivot swing-axle rear suspension with semi-trailing arms, coil springs, and telescopic deCarbon shock absorbers. The front suspension consisted of wishbones, coil springs, telescopic deCarbon shock absorbers, and an anti-sway bar. The deCarbon

From 1963 to 1971, all 230, 250, and 280SLs, with the exception of this one, were convertibles. In 1963, Pininfarina S.p.A. began design and construction of their '64 show cars to be displayed at the 51st International Paris Motor Show. It was to be a remarkable year. For Alfa Romeo, Pininfarina produced the Giulia 1600 Spider Veloce and for Ferrari a stunning trio, the 275 GTS Spider, 275 GTB Berlinetta, and 330 GT 2+2 Coupe. On their own stand, Pininfarina displayed what they described as two "world novelties" the Ferrari 500 Superfast Coupé and 230SL Mercedes Special Coupé.

ABOVE: The 600 was the most lavishly appointed production automobile ever manufactured by Daimler-Benz—and among the most expensive. With one notable exception, the 600 was built in three basic forms: the short-wheelbase Limousine, the longer-wheelbase Pullman Limousine (in four and six-door versions), and the similar but convertible-top Landaulet. This latter was the rarest series—and the most imposing. With its rear quarter roof lowered, the Landaulet was a parade car without equal. A mere fifty-nine examples were built, ten of which had a longer top. Nearly as rare and nearly as impressive were the massive six-door Pullman Limousines, 428 of which were produced. The short-wheelbase, four-door 600 Limousine was made in the greatest number, 2,190.

RIGHT: Coachwork was built at the Sindelfingen Werke. Each body was hand-crafted, much in the same philosophy as the 770 Grosser Mercedes and 540K models built by Sindelfingen in the 1930s. Interior dimensions were larger than those of any other contemporary limousine. Riders were cosseted by hand-sewn leather upholstery, luxurious wool carpeting, and hand-finished, grain-matched wood veneers for the dash, rear compartment, and door trim.

shocks were replaced by Bilsteins on the 250SL and the 280SL.

Though the 230, 250, and 280SLs never achieved true sports car status among enthusiasts, they raced past their predecessors in sales. From 1963 to 1971, Mercedes-

Benz sold 48,912 SLs. During that eight-year span they became more prevalent at country clubs, less prevalent at rallies and virtually nonexistent on the track.

Mercedes-Benz 600

Blending luxury with dependability and performance, the Mercedes-Benz 600 was simply the world's finest luxury car.

Introduced to the motoring world in 1963, the 600 is undoubtedly one of Mercedes' great postwar achievements. Here were luxury and performance inspired by that of the great 770 Grosser Mercedes of the 1930s. Like its revered predecessor, the 600 was built for an exclusive clientele of royal and wealthy owners, and then only in limited numbers.

In its 18-year life span, from August 1963 to June 1981, the longest for a single Mercedes-Benz model, only 2,677 cars were produced. Production of the 600 ran highest in 1965, when 345 limousines and sixty-three pullmans were built. The last 600 built, a short-wheelbase sedan, went straight into Daimler-Benz's museum collection.

Throughout its history the 600 has been the *voiture* of choice for pontiffs, politicians, and captains of industry. Among those who have enjoyed the use of a 600 have been King Hussein, Mao Tse-tung, Queen Elizabeth II, the Shah of Iran, Marshal Tito, Prince Rainier, the president of Rumania, and Pope Paul VI who commissioned a special Landaulet in 1966. A number of European governments have also used 600s as official cars.

All 600s were powered by a mechanically fuel-injected, ohc V-8 displacing 6.3ltr (386ci). The 90deg V-8, designated M100, had a compression ratio of 9.0:1, bore and stroke of 103mmx95mm, and peak output of 300hp at 4000rpm. Peak torque was a massive 434ft-lb at 3000rpm. This was Mercede's first production V-8 engine, and it was used exclusively in the 600 series until 1968.

Daimler-Benz Director of Passenger Car Development Rudolf Uhlenhaut, once said that the cost of building the 600 was of secondary importance. Virtually every part used in the cars was designed and built especially for that model. According to Uhlenhaut, the 600's design demanded "sufficient room for tall people; the best possible suspension; low body roll while cornering; a wide range of adjustability for all seats; well functioning ventilation, heating and air conditioning; silent operation of

The 300SE Coupe was one of the most handsome of all '60s-era Mercedes. Almost identical to the 220SEb Coupe, the car was powered by a 3.0ltr inline six, similar in layout to that used in the 300SL sports cars, including a seven-main-bearing crankshaft, light alloy block, and cast-aluminum head. The main difference was in the fuel delivery. The 300SL had fuel injection directly into the cylinders, while the 300SE used a manifold-injection system.

the whole car, and power assistance for all manual operations."

In terms of performance, the criteria were no less demanding. The 600 would require good road-holding, precise power-assisted steering, reliable brakes, tires suited to continued high-speed driving, adequate acceleration, strong body construction, and interior safety measures.

Bringing the 600 to a stop was a sophisticated dual-circuit hydraulic power-disc-brake system consisting of separate front and rear units operated by compressed air.

The 600 was unlike any other car built. Its four-wheel independent and height adjustable suspension provided an uncompromised smooth ride for passengers under virtually all road conditions. Settings for the hydraulic shock absorbers could be varied from

LEFT: One of the most famous Mercedes-Benz models in the world, this 1968 220D is the famous million-mile car seen in Mercedes-Benz advertising some years ago. The diesel-powered sedan was driven by its owner, Edward Donaldson, to and from work every day for eleven years. A daily round trip of 254mi!

soft to firm via a three-position lever on the steering column. Should road conditions demand extra ground clearance, the car could be raised 2in.

The cars were equipped with a vast array of special convenience features such as central vacuum locking for doors and trunk. Hydraulics opened and closed the trunk lid, the power windows, the limousine divider window, the sunroof, the fuel filler door, and the Landaulet's top. The heating and ventilation system included a climate control that could be set individually for front and back compartments. Even the radio had a remote control unit in the rear allowing the passenger to set the stations and volume. An intercom was standard, the front and rear seats were hydraulically operated, and thirteen interior lights kept things well illuminated.

Options were limited only by practicality and the buyer's pocketbook. Indeed, where the 600s were concerned, Daimler-Benz spared no expense. These were the finest automobiles that money could buy—or build; the greatest Mercedes-Benz cars of the 1960s.

Interior treatment on the 300SE and all 300-series models was exquisite, with plush leather upholstery and luxurious wood veneers for the dashboard and instrument pod.

CHAPTER EIGHT

Changing With the Times:
Cars of the 1970s and 1980s

Each era in the automobile's early development is highlighted by a technological step forward. For example, Mercedes-Benz advanced from the brute force of the SSK to the refined styling, performance and suspension design of the 540K. Although postwar transitions are somewhat less obvious, one stands out.

280SE

In the fall of 1969, Daimler-Benz introduced the 280SE 3.5 convertible, which simultaneously marked the end of one era and the beginning of another. A rare achievement. The car combined the elegant old body style of the 1960s with a new V-8 engine destined to become the standard for the 1970s and beyond. Added to the car's inherent rarity and luxury, this makes the 280SE 3.5 one of the most sought-after Mercedes-Benz models of recent times.

Until the 280SE 3.5, the only Mercedes-Benz V-8 available was the 6.3ltr engine used in the refined 600 series and the 300SEL 6.3. Historically, Daimler-Benz had tuned 4- and 6-cylinder engines to power their passenger cars. Though smaller than the V-8s in many American cars, Daimler-Benz sixes produced nearly the same power by revving much higher.

The 280SE 3.5 coupe was one of the most handsome cars of the '70s. Crisp, clean body lines were as elegant on the Coupe as the Cabriolet. Rear view of the 280SE 3.5 Coupe shows how well the design worked as a closed car. Wraparound back light gave drivers improved rear visibility and added a further touch of elegance to the Coupe's appearance.

LEFT: In a sense, Daimler-Benz was passing the torch to itself with the 280SE 3.5 Coupe and Convertible. Both were based on the previous 220SE body style introduced in 1961 at the re-opening of the Mercedes-Benz Museum in Stuttgart. Promptly tagged a collector's car by German motoring enthusiasts, the 220SE was an immediate success. Continuing the Teutonic appearance of Mercedes-Benz cabriolets dating back to the 1930s, the manual top's traditional tall stack of fabric consists of six layers of cloth, insulation, and padding—a sandwich up to 1-1/2in thick—supported by a steel framework concealed from view by a full interior headliner. Each top required more than 16hr of hand assembly. *Kurt Hillgruber*

With the new 3.5 V-8, the air-fuel mixture was compressed at a ratio of 9.5:1, allowing the compact engine to develop a stunning 230hp—more than 1hp per cubic inch! From the start it was clear that the 3.5's displacement could easily be expanded; the engine later evolved into the M117 that powered the 450SE/SEL and contemporary SL models, and its descendants can still be found in some Mercedes models.

The 3.5 V-8 filled the gap between the 3.0ltr sixes and the 6.3ltr V-8. Its modest size and weight allowed the engine to fit the mature 280SE chassis and provide it with youthful vitality. Despite the convertible's 110in wheelbase, overall length of 196.2in, and weight of 3,640lb, it could achieve 60mph from a standstill in 9.3sec and reach 130mph. Although not in the same league as the 6.3, straight-line performance was comparable to that of many European sports cars.

The 3.5 rode atop a fully independent coil-spring suspension with disc brakes at each wheel and an optional limited-slip differential. The convertible avoided the torsional flexing of most open cars by using a strengthened chassis with additional steel cross-braces below the leading edge of the rear seat, extending rearward under the trunk. On rough roads, body shudder and cowl shake were virtually nonexistent. Of all Mercedes-Benz models, this was perhaps the most perfect example of a luxury touring car ever to come from Germany.

350SL and 450SL

When the time came to introduce another SL, Mercedes-Benz once again started with a clean sheet

Leather lined most of the 280SE 3.5's cabin, wrapping the orthopedically correct seats (with vented surfaces for summer comfort) and covering the door panels, sun visors, instrument panel—even the glove box interior! All hides were hand-selected, measured, and crisply tailored in the Sindelfingen leather shop. A full array of luxury features included air-conditioning, power windows, reclining front seats with adjustable headrests and individually adjustable front center armrests, and a four-speaker Becker Europa AM/FM radio.

of paper. The 450SL was truly the first car to break traditional lines. There was no discrete caste among owners, the sporty two-seater appealed equally to gray-haired, Brooks Brothers-suited executives on Madison

LEFT: Despite a worldwide oil embargo, an economic recession, and a price tag twice that of most well-equipped Cadillacs ($12,500), in the early '70s, 450SLs were selling as fast as Mercedes-Benz dealers could get them. Seemingly overnight, it had become one of the most popular cars in America.

Uhlenhaut, Karl Wilfert, and Paul Bracq, as a 170 Diesel Sedan was from a 600 Pullman Limousine.

The 350SL, which was powered by an alloy 3.5ltr V-8, and the 450SL which followed in 1973, equipped with a more powerful 4.5ltr V-8, com-

Easy to read dials and gauges, the largest being the speedometer and tach, were artfully set into the dashboard with the driver's view in mind. Indeed, print

ads of the day touted "ergonomics" as a key design philosophy long before the word became a sales cliché.

Avenue and long-haired, Levi-clad rock stars on Sunset Strip, to both men and to women. As a two-place sports car, this was the Mercedes for all seasons. The 450SL's season—which lasted for a decade—began in 1971 when it was first introduced as the 350SL. By name, the cars were heir to the original 300SL coupes and roadsters of the 1950s and '60s, yet in image, as far from the sporty two-seaters pioneered by Rudolf

bined for the first time in a Mercedes-Benz model sports-car performance and handling, with a measure of luxury that had previously been reserved for Mercedes sedans.

The new 350/450SLs, however different from their predecessors, continued traditions established in 1957 with the 300SL Roadster—the choice of either a fabric convertible top or a removable hardtop,

LEFT: With the 450SL and SLC, Daimler-Benz defied "American" sales tradition. Detroit philosophy had been to offer a list of options as long as a car's wheelbase. Not so Daimler-Benz. The sporty two-seat convertible came equipped with virtually every feature as standard equipment. The list included air-conditioning, four-wheel disc brakes, automatic transmission, electric windows, a Becker AM/FM stereo, vacuum central door locks, automatic radio antenna, leather interior, removable hardtop, radial tires and styled steel wheels, even a tool kit and a glove-box flashlight.

a sweeping open grille with the Mercedes-Benz star and barrel, and seating for just two.

The 350/450SL chassis measured 96.9in, and was greater both in wheelbase and overall length, at 172.4in, than the 280SL it replaced. This provided additional interior room to accommodate the installation of air conditioning up front and occasional seating in the rear—although the car was still considered a two-place convertible.

The car was not only larger in physical dimensions, but in structural design and overall weight as well. The bodies were wider (70.5in) to accommodate door guard beams federally mandated for the American market and to cover wider section tires on a front/rear track of 57.2 and 56.7in, respectively. Bodied in steel, rather than aluminum, the new SL weighed in some 350lb heavier than its predecessor, yet could clock 0–60mph in an average of 9sec, thanks to a potent 190hp from the fuel-injected 3.5ltr double-overhead-camshaft (dohc) V-8.

The 450SL and SLC shared virtually identical styling; the longer wheelbase length (added from behind the door to the rear wheel arch) wasn't that obvious. The SLC designation dates back to 1971, when the first models to offer a longer wheelbase, more interior room and a fixed top were introduced. The SLC was by design contrary to the image Mercedes-Benz had established in 1957 when the 300SL Roadster eased the Gullwing off the road. *Bob Reinfried collection*

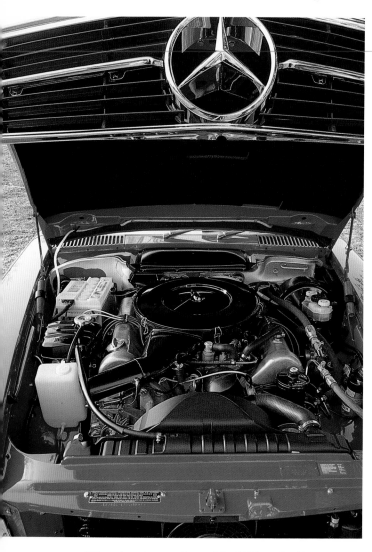

When American versions of the 350SL arrived in 1971, they were already equipped with the new 4.5ltr version of the engine and badged 350SL 4.5. In 1972, the cars were officially rebadged as the 450SL. American versions came equipped standard with a 3-speed automatic transmission. *Henry Seaggs collection*

When American versions of the 350SL arrived in 1971, they were already equipped with the new 4.5ltr version of the engine and badged 350SL 4.5. In 1972, the cars were officially rebadged as the 450SL. American versions came equipped standard with a 3-speed automatic transmission. A 4-speed automatic

NEXT PAGE: When the 450SEL 6.9 finally arrived in the U.S. market in 1977, it proved worth the wait. The car had been on sale in Europe since 1975, but had been considered inappropriate for the U.S. market during the gas crisis. Although almost indistinguishable from the standard 450SEL, the 6.9 was fitted with slightly larger bumpers than those of other U.S.-equipped models. Apart from that and the modest 6.9 badge on the trunk lid, all that differed went unseen and unheard. But it was definitely felt when you applied pressure to the accelerator.

was available in Europe as was a manual gearbox. Neither were offered on U.S. spec models. The ultimate 450SL was the European version, which had an output of 220hp, versus 190hp in U.S. trim.

Arguably the most civilized sports car ever built, the Mercedes-Benz 450SL also became one of the most successful. Through 1989, the car has carried eight different engines under the badge designations 280/300/350/380/420/450/500 and 560, accounting for an astonishing 237,287 vehicles sold worldwide, more than all other Daimler, Benz, and Daimler-Benz sports models put together since the company's inception.

450SEL

To the chagrin of many muscle car owners who came upon a 450SEL 6.9 in the late 1970s, Mercedes-Benz was flexing a few muscles of its own. The 6.9 was the ultimate sports sedan, a no-holds-barred, cost-be-damned automobile.

Apart from the more formal 600, the 6.9 was the best of the best, offered to those who would pay upward of $50,000 to purchase one of only 1,816 such cars produced for the U.S. market. In all, Daimler-Benz built 7,380 examples of the 6.9 from September 1975 to May 1980, although sales in this country were limited to the 1977 through 1979 model years.

The 6.9 enjoyed one of the largest powerplants available anywhere. The engine was derived from the M100 series that powered the 600 Limousines and 6.3 models, however, the fuel injection system was updated to Bosch's third-generation, mechanically controlled, continuous-injection K-Jetronic. Dry sump lubrication, unusual in any road car, was another feature of this uncompromising high-performance motor. With a bore of 107mm (4.21in) and stroke of

82

In 1988, Mercedes-Benz introduced the stylish 300TE Station Wagon. Although family wagons had been Mercedes fare for years, the 300TE marked the first time Daimler-Benz offered a gasoline-powered model in the North American market. Replacing the venerable 300TD turbodiesel, the 300TE was powered by a 177hp 3.0ltr six, the same engine used in the 300E, 300CE, and 300SEL models of that period.

95mm (3.74in), the 6.9 displaced 6,834cc, or 417ci! These were numbers more commonly associated with Detroit's drag-racing muscle cars than luxurious four-door sedans. Thanks to its immense low-rpm strength, the 6.9 could get by with a 3-speed, torque converter automatic transmission and a 2.65:1 rear axle ratio, making the car smoother and quieter. A limited-slip differential was standard. Unleaded fuel, stored in a 25gal tank, fed the 8.0:1 compression engine. In U.S. trim, the 6.9 developed 360ft-lb of torque at a remarkably low 2500rpm.

The 6.9 was engineered to be a true driver's car, albeit a really big one! Imagine the power of 6.9ltr, capable of moving this board room on wheels—one that could accommodate five adults in quiet, comfortable surroundings—from zero to 60mph in 8.2sec and on to a top speed of 137mph. Closing out the decade of the 1980s for Mercedes-Benz, the 450SEL 6.9 proved to be an automobile worthy of many superlatives, but needing none.

In the fuel conscious '80s, one of the best-selling models in the Mercedes-Benz line, at least in the U.S. market, was the 300SD turbodiesel. Until diesel emissions were ruled excessive by the California Air Resources Board (CARB), the 300SD was one of the top sellers in the state.

The S-Class cars were the classiest way to get from point A to point B throughout the 1980s. Models modified by AMG with fender flares, rocker panel treatments, air dams, deck-lid wings, monochromatic paint schemes, and specially tuned engines ruled the boulevards from Los Angeles to Manhattan.

CHAPTER NINE

The Second Hundred Years:

The 1990s and Beyond

Continually improving quality and performance is no mean feat, but Daimler-Benz continues to reinvent itself every decade, and in the '90s, it appears as if the company is going to reinvent the automobile as well.

First, let us take a brief look at the cars that started off the decade in high fashion. The most important was the new SL series, introduced in 1990 and '91 as the 300SL and 500SL. Drawing on the historic 300SL name for the first time in more than 30 years, Daimler-Benz focused on the image of the great Gullwings and roadsters from the 1950s and '60s. The 1995 versions, now designated SL320, SL500 and SL600—a historic change in itself putting the letters before the numbers for the first time—feature 6-, 8-, and 12-cylinder engines, respectively, and styling similar to the 1990 AMG version of the car, which featured more pronounced front and deck-lid spoilers, side skirts, and rear valance.

Designed to blend into the existing lines of the 1990 500SL, body components used by AMG were made out of PU-Rim, the same rubber/plastic material used by Mercedes-Benz on the lower body side panels, giving the AMG pieces the same exterior finish. Although the changes are hard to see, especially on a black car, they are both aesthetically and aerodynamically functional, providing the SL with an even sportier stance at rest and modestly improved high-speed stability. Adding to the car's functional attributes were 17in AMG three-piece modular racing wheels, 17x8in front, 17x10in rear, wrapped with Bridgestone 235/45x17in and 275/40x17in rubber, respectively.

More than a century of progress is depicted by the 1886 Benz Patent-Motorwagen, 1954 Mercedes-Benz 300SL Gullwing Coupe, and 1990 500SL Roadster. (Photographed at the 1990 Mercedes-Benz car show at Fashion Island, Newport Beach, California.)

Mechanically, AMG tuning for the SL offered a number of options, including a new rear differential gear set, which changed ratios from 2.65 to 3.27 and cut better than half a second off 0–60 times. AMG sport exhaust systems added 7–8hp, and the ultimate option, a 6ltr "exchange" motor, delivered 381hp compared to the stock 5.0ltr's 322hp. An AMG-powered 500SL could run from 0 to 60 in 5sec flat. It could also break the bank. The new 6ltr engine, including the trade-in of your stock 5ltr, was an estimated $25,000. The body treatment, rear differential, wheels, and tires, added another $18,000. For the privilege of making Porsches and Ferraris eat Daimler dust, SL owners paid up to $45,000 above the $91,000 base price for a 500SL in 1990. For 1995, buyers will pay in excess of $120,000 for the factory's high-performance V-12 SL600.

The Daimler-Benz product line for the 1990s is the most extensive since the '30s, when the company offered models in virtually every price range and classification from economical diesel sedans to luxurious touring cars. Today's version of that legacy spans from the C-Class 220 sedan, priced at around $30,000, to the $130,000 S600 sedan. In between are some of the most varied and interesting models in the company's 110-year history.

Improving upon the 190 series introduced in the 1980s, the Mercedes-Benz C-Class, which made its debut in 1994, has become one of the most successful new models in Daimler-Benz history. The stylish sedans are offered in a base C220 model equipped with a 2.2ltr 4-cylinder engine, or the C280 version powered by a 2.8ltr 6-cylinder engine.

The Mercedes-Benz E-Class has set new standards, virtually rewriting the book on luxury cars in the $40,000–50,000 price range. The most diversified series in the Mercedes-Benz product line, E-Class models range from the 6-cylinder E320 sedan, coupe, station wagon, and cabriolet—the first convertible sedan since the 1971 280SE 3.5—to the V-8 powered E420 sedan, and E300 diesel. The E300 is another Daimler-Benz benchmark, being the first to utilize four-valve-per-cylinder technology in a passenger-car

The greatest evolution of the Mercedes-Benz automobile may well be the forthcoming A-Class, a small, sub-compact Mercedes. The innovative concept, currently under the project name *Studie A,* utilizes front-wheel drive and a novel bodywork design that places all of the running gear—engine, transmission, suspension, fuel tank, and so on—beneath the floor of the vehicle, thus leaving an entirely open passenger compartment from front to rear with the usable space of a C-Class sedan.
Photo courtesy Mercedes-Benz North America

diesel engine, and establishing a record for mileage at 32mpg with a cruising range of 750mi between fill-ups.

The S-Class remains the flagship of the Mercedes-Benz line with a total of seven models, ranging from the V-8 powered S320 sedan to the stunning

The A-Class will measure slightly more than 11ft in overall length on a wheelbase of just 90.9in, the body comprised of steel, aluminum, and composites, with a curb weight of only 1,573–1,617lb. Providing optimum road handling, the four-passenger sedan will utilize McPherson struts, coil springs, and gas shocks in front and a composite link rear axle with coil springs and gas shocks. Power will initially be provided by either a 1.2ltr 3-cylinder turbodiesel engine or an optional 1.2ltr 3-cylinder gas engine. Unique 155/70 R15 tires manufactured with a special rubber mixture and tread pattern reduce rolling resistance by 30 percent, further contributing to the fuel economy estimates. *Photo courtesy Mercedes-Benz North America*

V-12 powered, long-wheelbase S600, the most luxurious Mercedes since the fabled 600 series produced from 1964 to 1981.

The 1995 models represent the culmination of more than a century of engineering and design evolution, from the first single-cylinder engine that powered the 1886 Patent-Motorwagen to the latest electronically-controlled, 48-valve, dohc V-12 powering the SL600. These, however, are *today's* cars, and what we have chosen to do in this final chapter is to look ahead to the late 1990s and into the next century.

A-Class Cars

The greatest evolution of the Mercedes-Benz au-

The 1997 Mercedes-Benz SLK Roadster styling is based on the current SL320 body but with more compact exterior dimensions and a pronounced wedge shape, with short front and rear overhang. The front of the car is characterized by an SL-style grille incorporating the traditional three-pointed star, while the upswept headlights and integrated turn signal lights reveal a dynamic interplay between design innovation and Mercedes history. *Photo courtesy Mercedes-Benz North America*

tomobile may well be the forthcoming A, Class, a small, sub-compact Mercedes. The innovative concept, currently under the project name *Studie A* utilizes front-wheel drive and a novel bodywork design that places all of the running gear—engine, transmission, suspension, and fuel tank—beneath the floor of the vehicle, thus leaving an entirely open passenger compartment from front to rear with the usable space of a C-Class sedan. Known as a "two-tier" assembly, this concept not only places all of the mechanical components beneath the passenger compartment, but allows the occupants to be positioned in the upper section in such a way that they are fully protected by the frame of the car in the event of a collision. According to Daimler-Benz engineers, the A-Class will meet the same safety requirements as any other sedan bearing the three-pointed star.

In addition to the front-, rear-, and side-impact protection afforded by the design of the four-door A-Class sedan, the driveline design adds even greater passenger safety. Mercedes claims that 75 percent of all accident injuries occur when drivetrain components are shoved into the passenger space. During a frontal collision in the A-Class, the engine and transmission would slide under the floorpan and below the passenger compartment.

While this is a radical departure from traditional Mercedes-Benz lines, it is indicative of the company's future thinking. The A-Class proves that it is possible to incorporate traditional Mercedes qualities into a small car. According to Daimler-Benz, the A-Class represents completely new ideas now paving the way for a generation of novel vehicles. Market researchers spoke to more than 1,800 drivers in Europe, Japan, and the United States, asking them for ideas about the car of the future. According to that research, more than two-thirds of all small and sub-compact car owners were taken with the idea of a "small" Mercedes and considered such a car to be in keeping with the times, particularly in view of today's environmental and road problems.

When it goes into production, the four-door A-Class sedan will measure slightly more than 11ft in overall length on a wheelbase of just 90.9in. The body will be comprised of steel, aluminum, and composites, with a curb weight of only 1,573–1,617lb. Providing optimum road handling, the sub-compacts will utilize McPherson struts, coil springs, and gas shocks in front and a composite link axle with coil springs and gas shocks in the rear.

Power will initially be provided by either a 1.2ltr 3-cylinder turbodiesel engine or an optional 1.2ltr 3-cylinder gas engine. Both versions will utilize an innovative *continuously variable* automatic transmission with torque converter. Also in development is an electric induction motor producing 54hp, powered by a sodium/nickel chloride battery developed jointly by Daimler-Benz and AEG. Known as the ZEBRA battery, it will provide the A-Class with a range of 90–100mi on a single charge. Recharging time on household current is estimated at 6–12hr; however, Daimler-Benz says that the time will be considerably shortened with a special high-speed recharging station.

Although at present there are no plans to sell the A-Class in the United States, if public demand is great enough, and if government mandates for zero-emission vehicles are enacted beginning in 1998, the electric version might be considered practical for the U.S. market. It might then be likely that all three engines would be made available. Only time will tell.

SLK Roadster

A little closer to our shores is the SLK Roadster, which will be introduced to the U.S. market in early 1997. The sporty two-seater carries the 300SL's rich forty-year tradition skillfully merged with a contemporary design suited to the next century. The legendary SLK name—originally that of a supercharged 300SL race car tested in 1952—further emphasizes the historic ties to this new model. Two narrow "power domes" on the hood of the SLK pay further homage to the first 300SL Coupes and Roadsters.

The styling for the SLK is based on the current SL320 but with more compact exterior dimensions

Rather than having a soft top and detachable hardtop, the SLK will feature a fully automatic retractable hardtop that disappears behind the rear body panels in about 25 seconds, giving the small two-seater the best advantages of both the fabled 300SL Coupe and Roadster.

and a pronounced wedge shape. The front of the car is characterized by an SL-style grille and traditional three-pointed star, flanked by stylish upswept headlights and integrated turn signal lights.

There is an historical imperative for the SLK—the 190SL Roadster produced by Mercedes-Benz from 1955 through 1963. Like the smaller, more affordable 190SL, which was powered by a 2.0 liter four-cylinder engine, the new and presumably less costly SLK Roadster will draw its *puissance* from a supercharged 2.3 liter, double overhead cam four-cylinder engine producing nearly 200hp. With a close-ratio five-speed gearbox, Mercedes claims a 0 to 60 time of 8.0 seconds in production trim.

Rather than having a soft top and detachable hardtop, the SLK will feature a fully automatic retractable hardtop that disappears behind the rear body panels in about 25 seconds. There will be no need to release any latches or install a boot when the top is down.

Mercedes is already busy retooling its Bremen manufacturing facility for an estimated annual production of 40,000 SLK Roadsters.

From where we stand, the second hundred years for Mercedes-Benz appears to be as promising as its first!

Index